OCCASIONAL PAPER **160**

G000112127

Fiscal Reforms in Low-Income Countries

Experience Under IMF-Supported Programs

**By a Staff Team led by George T. Abed
and comprising**

**Liam Ebrill
Sanjeev Gupta
Benedict Clements
Ronald McMorran
Anthony Pellechio
Jerald Schiff
Marijn Verhoeven**

INTERNATIONAL MONETARY FUND
Washington DC
March 1998

Library of Congress Cataloging-in-Publication Data

Fiscal reforms in low-income, countries : experience under IMF
 —supported programs / by George T. Abed . . . [et al.].
    p.   cm. — (Occasional paper; 160)
  "March 1998"
  ISBN 1-55775-717-8
    1. Fiscal policy—Developing countries.   2. Structural adjustment
(Economic policy)—Developing countries. I. Abed, George T.
II. International Monetary Fund. III. Series: Occasional paper
(International Monetary Fund) ; no. 160.
HJ1620.F573 1998
336.3'09172'4—dc21   97-52372
                                                CIP

Price: US$18.00
(US$15.00 to full-time faculty members and
students at universities and colleges)

Please send orders to:
International Monetary Fund, Publication Services
700 19th Street, N.W., Washington, D.C. 20431, U.S.A.
Tel.: (202) 623-7430   Telefax: (202) 623-7201
E-mail: publications@imf.org
Internet: http://www.imf.org

recycled paper

Contents

**Figures
Section**

The following symbols have been used throughout this paper:

. . . to indicate that data are not available;

n.a. to indicate not applicable;

— to indicate that the figure is zero or less than half the final digit shown, or that the item does not exist;

– between years or months (e.g., 1994–95 or January–June) to indicate the years or months covered, including the beginning and ending years or months;

/ between years (e.g., 1994/95) to indicate a crop or fiscal (financial) year.

"Billion" means a thousand million.

Minor discrepancies between constituent figures and totals are due to rounding.

The term "country," as used in this paper, does not in all cases refer to a territorial entity that is a state as understood by international law and practice; the term also covers some territorial entities that are not states, but for which statistical data are maintained and provided internationally on a separate and independent basis.

Preface

The reform of fiscal policies and institutions lies at the heart of structural adjustment in developing countries. Although the immediate aim of such reform is to reduce fiscal imbalances to achieve macroeconomic stability, the long-term goal is to secure more durable improvements in fiscal performance. To make revenue mobilization more efficient, for example, requires reforming the tax and tariff systems and their administration while, on the expenditure side, fiscal consolidation calls for reorienting public spending from current consumption toward growth-promoting investment in physical infrastructure and in social and human capital.

This study reviews the fiscal reform experience of 36 low-income developing countries that undertook macroeconomic and structural adjustment in the context of the IMF's Structural Adjustment Facility (SAF) and Enhanced Structural Adjustment Facility (ESAF) during the period 1985–95. It was carried out in conjunction with a more comprehensive assessment by IMF staff of the Policy and Development Review Department entitled *The ESAF at Ten Years: Economic Adjustment and Reform in Low-Income Countries*. Against the objectives set out in the programs, the study seeks to assess how far these countries have succeeded (a) in reforming their tax systems and institutions and in achieving programmed revenue targets, and (b) in reducing government absorption while shifting expenditures toward more productive activities. The paper concludes that although notable progress has been made on all fronts, much more needs to be done. More important, it extracts both from the aggregate analysis and from the case studies more specific conclusions and, it is hoped, instructive lessons for program design.

The study is the result of a considerable collaborative effort by the staff of the IMF's Fiscal Affairs Department. The authors are indebted to numerous colleagues but especially to Julio Escolano, Reint Gropp, Kristina Kostial, and Janet Stotsky, for their helpful comments on and significant contributions to various drafts; to Alexandros Mourmouras, Zeljko Bogetic, and Ludger Schuknecht for their thorough preparation of case studies; and to Manfred Koch and Keiko Honjo for the collection and organization of data. Diane Cross provided valuable editorial assistance while Asegedech WoldeMariam and Tarja Papavassiliou shouldered the enormous task of data manipulation with great skill and precision. Administrative support was ably provided by Meike Gretemann, Larry Hartwig, Leda Montero, Amy Deigh, and Nezha Karkas. J.R. Morrison of the External Relations Department edited the paper and coordinated production of the publication.

The opinions expressed in the paper are, of course, those of the authors and do not necessarily reflect the views of the IMF or of its Executive Directors.

1 Introduction and Summary

Since 1986 the International Monetary Fund has supported the adjustment programs of its low-income members with loans on highly concessional terms through two arrangements, the Structural Adjustment Facility (SAF) and the Enhanced Structural Adjustment Facility (ESAF) (Box 1). These facilities rest on two premises: first, that macroeconomic stabilization and structural reform of economic systems and institutions complement each other and second, that both are needed for economic growth with external viability.

At the heart of structural adjustment undertaken by developing countries lies the fiscal component of the program. Sound fiscal policy fosters macroeconomic stability. For one thing, sound fiscal policies work against inflation, which is important given the relatively limited financial intermediation in most SAF/ESAF countries and the associated potential for budget deficits to be monetized. Moreover, well-designed revenue and expenditure reforms may directly promote growth as well as enhance the economy's supply-side response.[1] More efficient revenue mobilization, for example, can fund needed public goods and services and help cut fiscal imbalances as well as promote investment and growth by reducing the adverse allocational effects of the tax system. On the expenditure side, more cost-effective public programs free resources for better uses, and changes in the composition of public spending can reorient public resources away from current consumption and toward growth-promoting investment in physical infrastructure and in social and human capital.

This paper briefly reviews aggregate fiscal developments, particularly those concerning the fiscal deficit and its financing. It focuses, however, on developments in the levels and composition of revenue and expenditures, and on reforms in revenue and expenditure policies and administration in the context of SAF/ESAF-supported programs. Thus, although much of the analysis takes place at a relatively disaggregated level, the policies described were generally guided by broad objectives of fiscal sustainability and other macroeconomic considerations. Finally, to keep the analysis manageable, the treatment of "revenue" and "expenditures" does not specifically address quasi-fiscal operations that, in some cases, may be significant.

As regards the methodology, we analyze revenue and expenditures on two levels. On one level, the analysis presents an aggregated overview of the experience of all 36 SAF/ESAF countries in the sample during 1985–95 (Box 2).[2] On another level, we examine the experiences of individual countries (summarized in Boxes 3–10). In the aggregated analysis, we review the program targets for the overall levels of revenue and expenditures and their individual components (generally as a percentage of GDP) using widely accepted best practices in tax and expenditure policy. We then compare the targets with outcomes before and after program initiation. Differences between targets and actuals are then analyzed to shed light on the reasons for the "success" or "failure" to achieve prescribed targets. We also review the longer-term impact of the adjustment efforts of SAF/ESAF countries by comparing revenue and expenditure outcomes in the period just before program initiation to those in the latest year (1994 or 1995) for which data were available.

The targets used for analysis are the latest revised annual targets for programs agreed to by the IMF and the countries' authorities, although estimates based on the original, unrevised annual targets are also reported. Most programs also established targets for the next three years at the time of initial approval. These targets generally cover macroeconomic indicators such as the overall deficit, and sometimes revenue or expenditures, although rarely their components. Thus, the choice of annual targets reflects both the absence of the necessary details in the original three-year-ahead targets, and a concern that any detailed three-year projections that did exist were highly tentative. However, for countries for which data are available, revenue and expenditure

---

[1]See Mackenzie, Orsmond, and Gerson (1997).

[2]Note that fiscal data for these countries were not always available in the needed detail for all periods considered; thus, the analysis was based, in some instances, on a smaller sample.

Box 1. SAF/ESAF: A Concessional Facility to Assist Poorer Countries

The IMF's Executive Board established the Enhanced Structural Adjustment Facility (ESAF) in 1987 to better address the macroeconomic and structural problems faced by low-income countries. It offers loans with lower interest rates and for longer terms than the typical IMF market-related arrangements. The principal objectives are to promote balance of payments viability and foster sustainable long-term growth. Although the objectives and features of the ESAF are similar to those of its predecessor, the Structural Adjustment Facility (SAF), set up in 1986, the ESAF was expected to be more ambitious with regard to macroeconomic policy and structural reform measures. The IMF no longer makes disbursements under the SAF.

ESAF loans are disbursed semiannually (as against quarterly for regular IMF stand-by arrangements), initially upon approval of an annual arrangement and subsequently based on the observance of performance criteria and after completion of a mid-term review. ESAF loans are repaid in 10 equal semiannual installments, beginning 5½ years and ending 10 years after the date of each disbursement. The interest on ESAF loans is 0.5 percent a year. By contrast, charges for stand-by arrangements are linked to the IMF's Special Drawing Right (SDR) market-determined interest rate, and repayments are made within 3¼ to 5 years of each drawing. A three-year access under the ESAF is up to 190 percent of a member's quota. The access limits of stand-by arrangements are 100 percent of quota annually and 300 percent cumulatively.

An eligible member seeking to use ESAF resources develops, with the assistance of the IMF and the World Bank, a policy framework paper (PFP) for a three-year adjustment program. The PFP, updated annually, sets out the authorities' macroeconomic and structural policy objectives and the measures that they intend to adopt during the three years. The PFP also lays out the associated external financing needs of the program, a process that is meant to catalyze and help coordinate financial and technical assistance from donors in support of the adjustment program.

Performance during the first year of an ESAF arrangement is usually monitored by quarterly quantitative and structural benchmarks that reflect the program's key elements. Quantitative benchmarks typically include monetary, fiscal, international reserves, and external debt variables, whereas structural benchmarks typically cover major institutional reforms, such as in the areas of public enterprise, the financial sector, structural fiscal policy, or tax and expenditure management. For the midterm review, the semiannual quantitative benchmarks usually serve as performance criteria, although key structural reforms may also be included. Currently, 79 countries are eligible for ESAF loans; at end-April 1997, 35 ESAF arrangements were in effect, with cumulative commitments totaling SDR 8.8 billion (about $12 billion)—of which SDR 7.2 billion (about $8 billion) had been disbursed.[1]

---

[1]The SDR, an international reserve asset created by the IMF and allocated to its members since 1970, is the IMF's unit of account. Its value is determined by the market-exchange rates of a basket of five currencies—the U.S. dollar, the deutsche mark, the French franc, the Japanese yen, and the pound sterling.

---

outcomes are also compared to the initial three-year targets.

To take account of the broader social impact of government spending, this paper also analyzes trends in SAF/ESAF countries' expenditures on education and health and changes in social indicators.

The principal findings on the overall fiscal performance and revenue and expenditure policies and performance are summarized below.

Major Findings on Overall Fiscal Performance

Programs envisaged relatively modest adjustments in the overall fiscal balance—on average, the overall fiscal deficit was slated to decrease about 1 percentage point of GDP from the preprogram year. Programs sought greater change in the financing of deficits, aiming to shift away from domestic financing and the accumulation of payment arrears toward foreign financing (most of which was highly concessionary). On average, programs targeted an annual reduction in payment arrears of 0.8 percent of GDP.

During the program periods significant progress was made with fiscal consolidation, with fiscal deficits falling most dramatically in those countries where, on average, initial deficits were highest. For example, in countries classified as having high initial deficits (see Box 2 for definitions), the average overall fiscal deficit shrank from 13.8 percent of GDP in the preprogram year to 9.5 percent of GDP in the most recent year. Also, there was a broad movement away from domestic financing, by an average of 2.1 percent of GDP, but the pattern of financing did not shift as much as anticipated. The annual accumulation of arrears fell less than programmed.

While countries, on average, met the targets for the overall deficit, outcomes varied considerably by region. Transition countries outperformed expectations (albeit from excessively high initial deficits), economic performance in Asian and African coun-

Box 2. SAF/ESAF Sample Countries and Definitions

Africa	Europe and Central Asia
Benin	Albania
Burkina Faso	Kyrgyz Republic
Burundi	Mongolia
Côte d'Ivoire	
Equatorial Guinea	**East and South Asia**
Gambia, The	Bangladesh
Ghana	Cambodia
Guinea	Lao People's
Kenya	Democratic Republic
Lesotho	Nepal
Madagascar	Pakistan
Malawi	Sri Lanka
Mali	Vietnam
Mauritania	
Mozambique	**Western Hemisphere**
Niger	Bolivia
Senegal	Guyana
Sierra Leone	Honduras
Tanzania	Nicaragua
Togo	
Uganda	
Zimbabwe	

The *preprogram year* is defined as the year preceding the first SAF/ESAF arrangement for each country.

Revenue ratios refer to revenue-to-GDP ratios unless otherwise stated.

Initial revenue efforts (ratios) were based on total revenue as a percentage of GDP, classified as follows: *low*, between 5 percent and 9.9 percent; *medium*, between 10 percent and 19.9 percent; and *high*, more than 20 percent.

High-deficit countries are those with deficits greater than 10 percent of GDP; *medium-deficit countries*, between 5 percent and 9.9 percent of GDP; and *low-deficit countries*, less than 5 percent of GDP.

tries fell slightly short of program objectives, and performance in Western Hemisphere countries fell significantly short of targets.

Major Findings on Revenue Mobilization

The analysis shows that improving the structure and administration of tax systems requires significant tax policy reforms, such as simplifying and rationalizing tariff and tax rates and introducing broad-based taxes on consumption, for example, value-added taxes (VATs). To improve tax and customs administration, these tax policy reforms need to be reinforced by appropriate institutional reforms.

SAF/ESAF-supported programs targeted, on average, a modest increase for both total revenue and tax revenue as a percentage of GDP. Programs in the CFA franc zone envisaged that revenue effort would remain unchanged. The revenue objectives indicated relatively large increases in the revenue-to-GDP ratio for countries with *low* initial revenue effort, smaller increases for *medium* initial effort countries, and virtually no increase for *high* initial effort countries (see Box 2 for definitions).

As regards program implementation, total revenue fell short of annual program targets by about 0.5 percent of GDP on average (somewhat greater when compared with the initial three-year targets), with adverse implications for expenditures. Underperformance was most notable in Africa. Latin American and transition countries, however, generally met revenue targets.

With respect to revenue components, the yields of consumption-based taxes and international trade taxes, although they rose during the program period, fell slightly short of targets, whereas those of income and profits taxes exceeded their targets by an annual average of 0.7 percent of GDP. Comparing the preprogram situation with the most recent data available shows that revenue components changed in the direction intended: tax revenue rose by 1.4 percent of GDP and nontax revenue declined by 0.4 percent. Half of the tax revenue gain was attributable to improved revenue mobilization from taxes on domestic goods and services.

A number of countries introduced or modified their VATs during program periods. Some of the VATs, however, contained undesirable features that led to mixed revenue results. In cases in which VATs conformed to widely accepted best practices, the results were generally positive.

Program countries that set specific benchmarks or prior actions for the reform of tariff policy and customs administration registered a stronger revenue performance than other program countries for international trade taxes. Insufficient data on revenue components precluded generalization of this result to other taxes.

Program shortfalls relative to targets were most pronounced for those countries with the lowest initial revenue effort. A number of these countries, however, did significantly improve their revenue performance, albeit less rapidly than programmed. Medium and high initial revenue effort countries performed better relative to targets.

Many SAF/ESAF participants that completed their programs on time also greatly improved their revenue yields. In general, however, the impact of interruptions in programs on revenue performance was ambiguous.

General Lessons for Tax Reform

Tax reform strategy should aim at simplifying and rationalizing tax and tariff structures and making greater use of broad-based consumption taxes, such as a modern VAT with, ideally, a single tax rate in the 15–20 percent range, a threshold to exclude small businesses, and the broadest possible coverage of goods and services.

Although some countries have resorted to short-term ad hoc revenue measures to meet immediate revenue needs, these measures should be viewed as temporary, and ESAF programs should remain centered on fundamental reforms in tax policy and administration.

Reform strategies should also seek to modernize tax and customs administrations, keeping in mind, however, that such institutional reforms take time to produce needed revenue gains.

The rise in revenue from international trade taxes in SAF/ESAF countries, contrary to long-term historical trends, is not necessarily inconsistent with structural reforms of the tax systems in SAF/ESAF countries over the average program period (about five years). While in some cases countries that collected more revenue from this source did so as a result of undertaking desirable macroeconomic or structural reforms (discussed below), others sought to safeguard revenue while domestic tax reforms were taking hold. This result has implications for the design and sequencing of tariff and tax reforms in the context of adjustment programs.

As noted above, some countries with low initial revenue effort failed to improve revenue performance as rapidly as envisaged. This result implies that programs designed to raise revenue over time in low-income countries should take account of administrative constraints. Generally, developing countries with low revenue-to-GDP ratios (around 10 percent) should emphasize efficient revenue mobilization as a key element in rectifying fiscal imbalances. On the other hand, at much higher revenue-to-GDP ratios (generally more than 20 percent), persistent macroeconomic imbalances would call for shifting fiscal consolidation efforts toward containing expenditures.

Major Findings on Expenditure Reform

Annual targets in SAF/ESAF programs have aimed, on average, to maintain total expenditure as a share of GDP while shifting the composition from current spending to capital spending. Relative to average spending in the three years preceding the program, these programs envisaged that capital expenditure would rise by an average 1.4 percentage points of GDP and that current spending would fall an average 2.2 percentage points of GDP. According to initial three-year-ahead targets, SAF/ESAF countries sought to reduce noninterest public spending by 1.9 percentage points of GDP.

Total expenditure averaged some 0.5 percent of GDP less than programmed, with lower-than-programmed spending traceable to shortfalls in revenue and in foreign financing. Revenue shortfalls led to lower-than-programmed capital expenditures in over three-fourths of the countries. Outcomes from the initial three-year-ahead targets deviated considerably more than those from annual targets.

Over the typical program period, SAF/ESAF countries succeeded in changing the composition of spending in the direction envisaged. The share of capital spending in the total increased and that of current spending declined, although changes often fell short of the extent envisaged.

Within current spending, the share of wages and salaries in GDP was, on average, slightly higher than targeted but substantially lower than in the pre-program period. The overall decline in wages and salaries as a share of GDP was due more to real wage shrinkage than to the employment cutbacks envisaged under civil service reforms.

The allocation of outlays by function changed significantly, with less spending on military, general public, and economic services (essentially subsidies and transfers) and more spending on education and health.

Expenditure management improved in a number of SAF/ESAF countries, aided by extensive technical assistance from the IMF. Shortcomings in expenditure management have persisted, however, and have impeded fiscal adjustment and structural reforms in many countries.

Temporary social safety nets were incorporated into many SAF/ESAF programs to mitigate the short-term adverse effects of price increases and reduced job opportunities. In some cases, implementation proved difficult because social policy instruments were lacking and targeting of benefits was imperfect. Evaluating the implementation and effectiveness of these safety nets suffers from insufficient data.

Countries with no program interruptions generally had lower expenditure-to-GDP ratios than programmed. Difficulties in timely completion of programs are linked to overruns in current outlays.

Education and health spending rose in real terms and in relation to GDP after the initiation of the first program in SAF/ESAF countries. Real annual spending per capita on education and health rose by

3.8 percent and 5.8 percent, respectively. In both cases, results varied considerably among countries. Key social indicators also improved in SAF/ESAF countries.

General Lessons for Expenditure Reform

Programs should incorporate explicit, monitorable quantitative targets for reductions in public employment. These targets should be based on actual numbers of workers rather than positions. Greater progress in this area will likely require larger input from the World Bank in support of civil service reform. In addition, programs should focus on a medium-term plan, rather than one-shot reductions, and on strengthening or creating institutions that ensure control over recruitment and the civil service payroll.

Considerable scope exists for increasing the level, efficiency, and benefit incidence of social spending. Progress in this area is currently constrained, however, by the limited data on functional categories of spending, particularly social spending. Thus, comprehensive and timely data on expenditures by function should be compiled and made available so that adjustment programs can incorporate targets that are realistic, easy to monitor, and supported by underlying analysis.

Social indicators in ESAF countries should be monitored on a continuous and systematic basis as they evolve.

The reform of budgeting and expenditure control systems should place greater emphasis on improving the quality of human capital, providing appropriate incentives for officials charged with carrying out the reforms and ensuring transparency and accountability. Programs should also consider making greater use of prior actions in this area.

Because revenue shortfalls often adversely affect expenditure composition and the accumulation of arrears, contingency measures on the expenditure side need to be considered systematically and a core budget of high-priority allocations that would be protected from ad hoc cuts specified.

Capital spending targets should be based on realistic expectations of the capacity for project implementation, and care should be taken to protect essential public investment from budget cuts.

Social safety net measures figure prominently in programs, but information concerning their impact on the targeted population groups is scarce. Greater effort should be made to follow up on these measures, particularly to ascertain whether programs are reaching their intended beneficiaries.

II Review of Fiscal Developments

The countries that seek support under the SAF and ESAF programs are typically those experiencing deep-seated macroeconomic and structural problems, often associated with persistent weak growth, high inflation, low rates of national savings, and fragile external positions. For example, during 1981–85, the average annual real per capita GDP growth in countries that later entered into ESAF arrangements was –1.1 percent, in contrast to 0.3 percent in non-ESAF developing countries. In addition, the annual inflation rates for prospective ESAF countries during this period averaged about 95 percent, and most ESAF countries—with the exception of those in the CFA franc zone and some in Asia—experienced significant and disruptive volatility in inflation rates.[3]

One way the economic imbalances in these countries in preprogram periods manifested themselves was in large and unsustainable fiscal deficits. The overall fiscal deficit for the sample of countries averaged 9.6 percent of GDP in the three years before adoption of a SAF/ESAF-supported adjustment program (Table 1). The primary (noninterest) deficit averaged 6.8 percent of GDP and the current deficit, a measure of public dissaving, averaged 1.6 percent of GDP during the same period. Imbalances were particularly large in the transition countries, where during the three-year preprogram period, the overall deficit averaged 11.1 percent of GDP while the primary and current deficits amounted to 10.2 percent and 3.4 percent of GDP, respectively (Appendix Table 11). Non-CFA franc zone African countries in the sample also experienced relatively large fiscal imbalances.

In the three-year preprogram period, approximately two-thirds of the financing of the overall deficits took the form of foreign grants and net foreign borrowing. This number is an average, however, and masks considerable variation among the countries in the sample. Non-CFA franc zone African as well as Asian and transition countries re-

lied relatively more on domestic financing (Appendix Table 12). Reliance on domestic bank financing depended on the capacity of the individual countries to tap alternative domestic sources without crowding out needed private sector activity. This capacity was quite limited, at least in the African and transition countries in the sample.

An important objective of the SAF/ESAF-supported programs was to bolster domestic savings—during 1981–85, gross national savings in SAF/ESAF countries averaged only 8 percent of GDP. As a practical matter, seeking such an improvement required efforts to increase public savings by reducing the current balance deficit. Consequently, the fiscal adjustment incorporated in SAF/ESAF programs typically envisaged a combination of deficit cutting and medium-term structural reform of government revenue and spending, the latter to place the fiscal accounts on a sounder basis over the long term. Successful fiscal adjustment was to contribute to reductions in inflation, in part, by limiting government recourse to domestic bank financing.

The extent of the fiscal adjustment envisaged in the typical SAF/ESAF program was modest in terms of the overall fiscal balance—the overall fiscal deficit was to decrease by about three-fourths of a percentage point of GDP, on average, from the three-year preprogram period average. Somewhat more ambitious adjustments were sought in the Asian and Western Hemisphere countries than in the African, and in those countries with relatively high initial fiscal deficits. Programs envisaged an average reduction in primary deficits of about 0.8 percent of GDP.[4]

Besides the deficit reduction targets, programs also set objectives for changing the mix of financing. Specifically, the SAF/ESAF programs envisaged that, in addition to attaining fiscal sustainability, the pattern of financing should shift away from domestic bank financing and the accumulation of arrears. This shift was meant to alleviate pressures on

---

[3]The data in this paragraph are drawn from International Monetary Fund (forthcoming).

[4]Note the sample of countries for which primary balance targets were available was smaller than the sample for the overall balance targets.

Table 1. Summary of Fiscal Objectives[1]
(In percent of GDP; averages of SAF/ESAF country samples)

	(1) Pre-program Year	(2) Average of Three Years Prior to Program	(3) Latest Year Actual[2]	(4) Average Program Target	(5) Average Actual During Program	(6)=(5)–(4) Average Program Actual Minus Target
Fiscal balances						
Overall balance	–9.8	–9.6	–7.6	–8.9	–8.9	—
Region						
Africa	–9.2	–9.7	–7.6	–8.4	–8.7	–0.3
CFA franc countries	–8.7	–8.7	–7.5	–8.0	–7.6	0.4
Other	–9.5	–10.3	–7.6	–8.6	–9.2	–0.7
Asia	–8.8	–9.1	–6.5	–7.4	–8.1	–0.7
Western Hemisphere	–5.4	–7.0	–5.4	–5.7	–7.5	–1.8
Transition economies	–14.7	–11.1	–9.3	–13.4	–11.2	2.2
Initial deficit[3]						
High	–13.8	–13.4	–9.5	–12.1	–11.4	0.6
Medium	–7.8	–7.8	–6.4	–7.0	–7.6	–0.6
Low	–4.3	–4.1	–5.7	–5.5	–5.9	–0.4
Primary balance	–6.8	–6.8	–4.2	–6.0	–5.8	0.2
Current balance	–1.9	–1.6	0.5	0.5	–0.1	–0.7
Financing	9.8	9.6	7.6	8.9	8.9	—
Foreign financing	6.7	6.0	6.8	9.9	8.2	–1.7
Foreign grants	3.0	2.7	3.0	4.1	3.5	–0.6
Net foreign borrowing	3.8	3.4	3.8	5.8	4.7	–1.1
Domestic financing (net)	3.0	3.4	1.0	–0.1	0.9	1.0
Of which: Financing from banking system	1.5	1.7	—	–0.8	–0.1	0.7
Arrears	—	0.2	–0.2	–0.8	–0.2	0.7

Sources: Country authorities; and IMF staff estimates.

[1]Averages calculated for total SAF/ESAF country sample excluding Guyana, where major revisions to GDP in the program years rendered comparisons, before and after, virtually meaningless.

[2]Latest year for which data are available.

[3]Countries divided into high, medium, and low initial deficit based on their average deficit for the three years preceding program adoption. High-deficit countries are those with deficits greater than 10 percent of GDP; medium, 5–9.9 percent; and low, less than 5 percent.

limited domestic financial resources and create room for expansion of private sector activity. Some of the most dramatic reductions in bank financing of the overall fiscal deficits were envisaged for the African countries, with an increasing share for concessional foreign financing. For the CFA franc zone countries, for example, net foreign borrowing was programmed to grow, on average, from 3.1 percent to 7.1 percent of GDP. In the case of the non-CFA franc zone African countries, reliance on bank financing was envisaged, on average, to decline by about 4.5 percentage points of GDP.

Turning to program outcomes, we found countries attained their targets for the overall deficit, on average, but again, outcomes varied considerably among regions. The overall fiscal deficits, on average, exceeded the program targets in both the non-CFA franc zone African and the Western Hemisphere countries. By contrast, the CFA franc zone and the transition

countries achieved better-than-programmed fiscal outcomes. Also notable is that the countries with high initial deficits overperformed (Mozambique, Albania, Lao People's Democratic Republic, and the Kyrgyz Republic), whereas those with low initial deficits failed to meet their overall deficit targets (Figure 1).

Over the typical program period, fiscal consolidation progressed significantly in SAF/ESAF countries. The average overall fiscal deficit fell from 9.6 percent of GDP in the three years before the program to 7.6 percent of GDP in the most recent year for which data are available. The reductions were most striking in those countries where the initial deficits were the highest—from an average of 13.4 percent of GDP in the three-year preprogram period to 9.5 percent of GDP in the most recent year. The non-CFA franc zone African countries cut their overall deficit from an average of 10.3 percent of GDP in the three-year preprogram period to 7.6 percent of GDP.

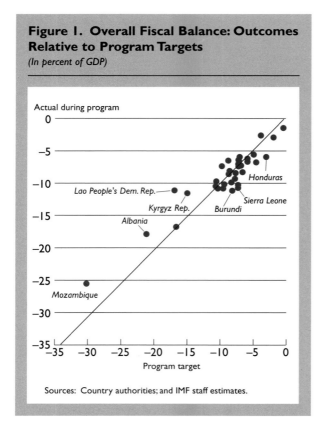

Figure 1. Overall Fiscal Balance: Outcomes Relative to Program Targets
(In percent of GDP)

Sources: Country authorities; and IMF staff estimates.

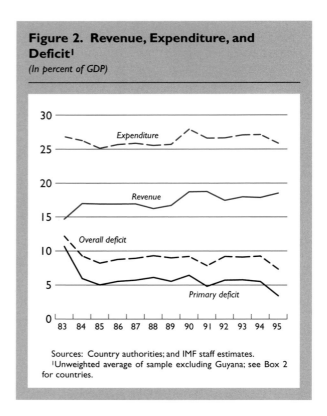

Figure 2. Revenue, Expenditure, and Deficit[1]
(In percent of GDP)

Sources: Country authorities; and IMF staff estimates.
[1]Unweighted average of sample excluding Guyana; see Box 2 for countries.

The bulk of the adjustment occurred on the revenue side, with the average revenue-to-GDP ratio increasing from under 15 percent in 1983 to about 18 percent in 1995 (Figure 2). Significant reductions in the overall and primary deficits of SAF/ESAF countries were achieved in the most recent years, when many adjustment programs were reinvigorated (as in the CFA franc zone following the 1994 currency devaluation) and when the policy and institutional reforms began to take hold (as in the transition countries).[5]

Although overall deficit targets were achieved on average, financing objectives were missed by a considerable margin as countries failed to reduce their reliance on domestic financing—partly because of shortfalls in foreign financing. Net foreign borrowing and foreign grants were both below target by the equivalent of 1.1 and 0.6 percentage points of GDP, respectively, while net domestic financing was about 1 percentage point of GDP above target. As pointed out in subsequent sections, the failure to mobilize as much foreign financing as anticipated may have

been a factor in the shortfall in meeting capital expenditure targets in SAF/ESAF countries.

There are differences in the regional patterns of financing outcomes. Although all regions experienced shortfalls in foreign financing, including in foreign grants, the CFA franc zone countries and the transition countries, in particular, experienced larger shortfalls in net foreign borrowing. However, for both of these groups, the shortfalls were not accompanied by a corresponding increase in domestic financing, indicating a likely buildup of arrears or incomplete fiscal accounting.[6] In contrast, in the non-CFA franc zone African countries the shortfall in foreign financing had its counterpart in greater-than-anticipated domestic financing. This differential response between the CFA and non-CFA franc zone African countries likely reflected the disciplining effect of a common central bank on domestic borrowing in the CFA franc zone, a role enhanced by the relatively less developed financial intermediation in the region. The combination of limited external financing and a regional central bank that pursued a tight monetary policy to support a fixed exchange rate meant that government expenditures could be financed only

---

[5]This improvement was also aided by the extension of SAF/ESAF programs to new countries that happened to have lower deficits relative to the current group mean at that time.

[6]The arrears data in Appendix Table 12 refer only to annual flows; the absence of adequate data on the stocks of arrears before and during programs precludes an accurate assessment of their role in fiscal consolidation.

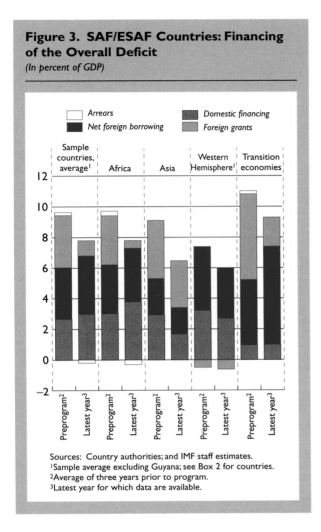

Figure 3. SAF/ESAF Countries: Financing of the Overall Deficit
(In percent of GDP)

Sources: Country authorities; and IMF staff estimates.
[1]Sample average excluding Guyana; see Box 2 for countries.
[2]Average of three years prior to program.
[3]Latest year for which data are available.

by tax revenue or the accumulation of arrears (central bank financing of the budget deficit is by statute limited to 20 percent of revenue). Indeed, the lack of domestic financing in the CFA franc zone countries also likely contributed to their above-mentioned modest overperformance on fiscal consolidation.

Although the pattern of financing did not shift as much as anticipated during program periods, there was broad movement away from domestic bank financing. This shift occurred in all regions, although relatively steeper declines occurred in the non-CFA franc zone African and the Western Hemisphere countries (Figure 3). Comparing the average from the most recent year for which data were available with the average of the three-year preprogram period shows that total domestic financing declined by 2.4 percentage points of GDP, the entire decline being traceable to lower domestic bank financing. The decline was 4.1 percentage points of GDP for countries with high initial fiscal deficits, of which 3.1 percentage points were attributable to reduced bank borrowing. On average, the SAF/ESAF countries reduced their payment arrears by 0.2 percent of GDP; however, this performance fell short of the targeted reduction of 0.8 percent of GDP per year. The slippage was particularly large in CFA franc zone countries—amounting to 2 percent of GDP.

As noted above, sustainable fiscal consolidation cannot be measured simply by the behavior of macroeconomic aggregates such as the fiscal deficit; systemic structural reforms must seek sustainable revenue mobilization and improved expenditure policy and management. The following sections discuss the structural reforms in the tax and expenditure systems in SAF/ESAF countries and assess their implications for improved economic performance.

III   Revenue Policy and Performance

Adjustment programs have often been initiated at times of fiscal stress, with initial efforts focused on alleviating fiscal imbalances that threatened macroeconomic stability. Although short-term measures, such as increased transfers from parastatals and temporary surcharges, often helped meet immediate revenue needs, these measures were generally unsuited to sustained revenue mobilization. Thus, an important aim of many SAF/ESAF programs has been to improve the structure and administration of tax systems to enhance efficiency and facilitate revenue mobilization.

Revenue Objectives and Program Targets

Accordingly, SAF/ESAF programs typically included tax policy and administrative reforms designed to broaden the revenue base, improve compliance, enhance equity, and reduce distortions stemming from existing complex and inefficient tax systems. Tax policy reforms typically included key elements from among the following measures:
- Introducing or strengthening a *broad-based consumption tax*, notably a VAT, preferably with a single rate (generally in the range of 15–20 percent) and minimal exemptions, with excise taxes levied at ad valorem rates and restricted to a limited list of products, principally petroleum products, alcohol, and tobacco. VATs and excises, where applicable, were to be applied equally to imports as well as domestic products.
- With domestic taxes, such as the VAT, assigned the primary revenue-raising role, setting *import tariffs* at a moderate-to-low average rate and limiting the dispersion of rates to reduce arbitrary and excessive effective rates of protection. Export duties were to be avoided.[7]
- With a view to ensuring administrative simplicity, among other things, reforming the structure

of the personal income tax through the introduction of limited personal exemptions and deductions; a moderate top marginal rate; an overall exemption limit that excludes persons with modest incomes; and extensive use of final withholding. Levying the *corporate income tax* at one moderate rate, preferably the same rate as the top marginal rate under the personal income tax, and making provisions such as depreciation allowances uniform across sectors, with minimal recourse to tax incentive schemes.
- Introducing a simplified (generally presumptive) tax regime for small businesses and the informal sector to bring these sectors into the tax net and to reduce the resources needed to administer the tax system.
- Forgoing some significant sources of nontax revenue, notably the arbitrary extraction of surpluses from parastatals, on the grounds they are volatile and generally unsustainable rent-based levies.[8]

SAF/ESAF countries typically faced significant problems in revenue collection owing to ineffective tax and customs administrations. Transition countries faced a special set of problems because revenue collection under centrally planned systems was not based on modern tax administration principles.[9] Hence, tax administration reforms, generally associated with modernization of systems and procedures as well as enhancement of institutional capacity, aim to place revenue collection on a permanently sounder basis. Simplification of the tax system through the tax policy reforms mentioned above provides strong support for subsequent administrative reforms. The usual reform approach stresses the adoption of effective procedures for taxpayer registration and education, collection enforcement and audit, computeriza-

---

[7]Without detracting from their inherent inefficiencies and distortionary effects, export taxes have at times been defended as expedients for income taxes in hard-to-tax sectors such as agriculture.

[8]Nontax revenue can still be an important component of a reformed tax system. For example, the user fees that would result from the appropriate commercialization of the supply of government services in areas such as education and health would count as nontax revenue.

[9]Revenue developments in transition economies are extensively reviewed elsewhere. For example, see Cheasty and Davis (1996).

tion and more effective management of taxpayer databases, the reorganization of tax and customs administrations along functional lines, and the institution of systems to promote the development of specialized skills among tax officials. This approach is often linked to the introduction of a VAT, which serves as a catalyst for the reform of the tax administration. Since the adoption of new procedures and organizational changes is complex and time consuming, a progressive approach needs to be followed so as not to overwhelm administrative capacity.

Clearly, not all countries undertaking structural adjustment in the context of SAF/ESAF programs were able to adopt all or most of these reforms, although many sought to reorient their tax systems in the general direction of these reforms by adopting those measures suited to their particular circumstances. Some actions taken in the context of SAF/ESAF programs, often in response to an urgent need to increase revenue, may have run counter to widely accepted notions of tax reform (see Box 3).

Even when reforms are implemented expeditiously, significant shifts in the structure of revenue happen slowly. The combination of the level of economic development and associated economic structure will define the tax system that typically emerges. In particular, it is only over the long term, as domestic productive capacity (and hence the domestic tax base) grows and broadens and as administrative capacities improve, that a major shift from reliance on international trade taxation to reliance on domestic taxation would be expected to occur. Moreover, in the short run, trends for revenue components can be misleading since, even with steady liberalization, many tariff reforms can have positive revenue effects. Reforms in this category include (1) the tariffication of quantitative restrictions; (2) the reduction or elimination of exemptions; (3) reduced incentives for smuggling through lower tariff rates; and (4) higher minimum tariff rates. In addition, customs revenue will probably be boosted by improved customs administration and increased imports, the latter often in response to devaluations, higher growth, and liberalization more generally.

Still, the successful implementation of a comprehensive program of structural reform in the tax area does not necessarily result in an immediate increase in the overall revenue-to-GDP ratio. Many reforms such as implementing VATs at their point of introduction are deliberately set to be broadly revenue neutral to bolster support for implementation; only over the medium-to-long term might revenue be expected to grow given the greater revenue buoyancy built into well-structured tax reforms. More fundamentally, the sample of countries covered in this review is heterogeneous with a number of countries already having relatively high tax-to-GDP ratios,

raising the issue that revenue objectives need to be related to some notion of the adequacy and efficiency of government spending and, more generally, the appropriate size of government, an issue beyond the scope of this paper.

Nonetheless, the authorities often need to make practical judgments on the appropriate balance between revenue and expenditure adjustment. Such judgments need to take into account the empirical evidence that the capacity of a country to raise revenue efficiently tends to rise with the level of income (per capita GDP). Although obviously depending on individual circumstances,[10] limited administrative capabilities and the economic structures of many developing countries (notably, the relatively larger size of difficult-to-tax agriculture and informal sectors) often imply a relatively narrow tax base. As a result, developing countries in the SAF/ESAF range of per capita incomes tend to find raising revenue beyond a certain level difficult. The unweighted average revenue-to-GDP ratio for the 36 SAF/ESAF countries was 18.1 percent in the latest year for which data are available (Appendix Table 13),[11] with only about one-third having revenue ratios in excess of 20 percent. The average performance is broadly comparable with that observed in other developing country groupings.[12] The empirical evidence, therefore, indicates that revenue ratios much in excess of 20 percent would likely strain the administrative capacity of most nontransition ESAF countries. Moreover, given the relative narrowness of the tax base and the inefficiencies of tax administration in many of these countries, tax ratios above this level would likely be highly distortionary. Accordingly, countries with a relatively low revenue ratio (about 10 percent of GDP) should have the capacity to raise their revenue ratios, through efficient revenue mobilization centered on tax reform, toward the 20 percent level over the medium to long term. On the other hand, countries with a revenue ratio much in excess of 20 percent that are confronting a need for fiscal consolidation would likely benefit from shifting the focus of policy actions toward expenditure containment. In all

---

[10]For example, a country with a large natural resource endowment may benefit from royalties and other nontax revenue, thus allowing it to sustain above-average revenue ratios with only modest tax effort.

[11]The (unweighted) average tax-to-GDP ratio was 15.4 percent. Details of the revenue composition of the 36 SAF/ESAF countries are shown in Appendix Tables 14–18.

[12]For example, for 1986–92, the revenue-to-GDP ratios for non-OECD Asian countries and non-OECD Western Hemisphere countries were an unweighted average of 18.9 percent and 19.7 percent, respectively. The corresponding ratio for the OECD was 34.3 percent (see Shome, 1995). For a historical comparative overview of this issue, see Tanzi and Schuknecht (1995).

Box 3. Revenues: Balancing Immediate Needs with Medium-Term Objectives

In many countries facing fiscal imbalances, near-term measures were used to mobilize revenue until major reforms of the tax system and its administration could take effect. While some of the near-term measures, such as targeted increases in user charges, had merit, others were merely expedient. Some examples of how the balance between these near-term and long-term measures was struck are provided by the cases of Albania, Kenya, and Mongolia.

Albania: Following a collapse in the revenue base— tax revenue declined from the equivalent of 42 percent of GDP in 1990 to 17 percent of GDP in 1992—the authorities endeavored to bolster revenue in the face of a large fiscal deficit. The immediate revenue measures included hikes in excise tax rates on petroleum products, alcoholic beverages, soft drinks, and tobacco; the introduction of an excise on coffee; an increase in the specific import duty for used cars; and an elimination of the exemptions from the turnover tax (for agricultural equipment and canned food). Recognizing the limited contribution of such measures to the longer-term objectives of tax reform, the authorities also focused on structural tax reforms aimed at improving the efficiency and buoyancy of the tax system. These objectives were to be achieved through the elimination of the export tax, the rationalization of customs duties (by reducing exemptions and adopting a three-tier structure with a standard tariff of 25 percent), and the broadening of the tax net to include land, livestock, and motor vehicles. Of particular significance, in July 1996 the authorities also replaced the turnover tax with a VAT.

Kenya: The fundamental fiscal objective of Kenya's ESAF program was the reduction of the budget deficit. Near-term revenue measures included discretionary tax changes and the introduction of user charges for health, education, transportation, and other services, with the objective of helping to finance improvements in the quality of government services. Structural tax reforms were designed to broaden the tax base and enhance the buoyancy of the tax system and included the phased replacement of the existing cascading sales tax with a uniform VAT. Reforms also encompassed changes to the tariff system to lower the average rate of effective protection, reduce the dispersion of rates, phase out export duties, and make the structure of international trade taxation more transparent. Authorities planned to introduce a presumptive tax of 5 percent on the value of gross sales of agricultural products to offset the revenue loss from the elimination of the export tax on coffee and tea.

Mongolia: Mongolia faced the prospect of containing fiscal pressures while also managing the difficult transition to a more market-oriented economy. Near-term measures to bolster revenue comprised introducing a 10 percent sales tax on imports and on domestic production, reducing the scope of customs exemptions for imports, and raising specific rates of the vehicle tax. Authorities sought additional revenue by introducing a measure to transfer to the budget windfall profits from sales of copper concentrate associated with the adoption of the new exchange rate system. Medium-term tax reforms included replacing the multirate turnover tax system with a single-rate sales tax that would initially be applied to the manufacturing sector but, over time, would be extended to other sectors; replacing quantitative import restrictions with an ad valorem tariff structure; simplifying the individual income tax rate schedule and exemptions; and lowering corporate profit tax rates.

---

cases, however, other factors may influence the desirable adjustment mix, such as the existing structure of the tax system, administrative capabilities, and debt-service demands.

Turning to program objectives, we found the average program target for total revenue was 18.8 percent of GDP compared with average actual total revenue in the preprogram year of 17.1 percent of GDP (Table 2).[13] The tax revenue target was, on average, 15.5 percent of GDP, compared with average actual preprogram year collections of 14.1 percent of GDP. Nontax revenue was projected to decline from an average preprogram year level of 3.0 percent to 2.7 percent of GDP. About 70 percent of the countries

projected an increase in the total revenue-to-GDP ratio, three-fourths an increase in the tax revenue ratio, and slightly more than half projected a decline in the nontax revenue ratio.[14]

An analysis of annual tax revenue targets according to *initial revenue effort* (Figure 4 and Appendix Table 19) indicates that SAF/ESAF countries with *low* initial revenue effort aimed for an increase in average tax revenue of 3.0 percentage points of GDP—from 6.2 percent in the preprogram year to a target of 9.2 percent, while a more modest increase was targeted for countries with *medium* initial revenue effort—from 12.2 percent to a target of 14.1 percent of GDP. For countries with *high* initial revenue effort, the programs targeted, on average, un-

---

[13]Comparisons are not made with the average revenue outturns for the three years preceding a program because the aggregate averages tend to be distorted by the high initial revenue levels of the transition economies during that period.

[14]Hereafter, unless otherwise stated, references to *revenue ratios* will be understood to be relative to GDP.

Table 2. Revenue: Summary of Program Targets[1]
(Averages of SAF/ESAF country samples)

	Average of Three Years Prior to Program	Pre-program Year	Average Program Target[2]	Target ≥ Preprogram Actual	Target < Preprogram Actual	Number of Countries[3]
	⟵――― In percent of GDP ―――⟶			Percent of countries		
Total revenue	18.1	17.1	18.8	69.4	30.6	36
Tax revenue	14.7	14.1	15.5	76.5	23.5	34
Of which:						
Taxes on domestic goods and services	5.2	4.9	5.7	56.5	43.5	23
Taxes on income, profits, and capital gains	4.8	4.4	4.6	54.5	45.5	22
Taxes on international trade	4.7	4.7	5.7	72.7	27.3	22
Nontax revenue	3.4	3.0	2.7	47.1	52.9	34

Sources: Country authorities; and IMF staff estimates.

[1]The disaggregated data on which this table is based can be found in Appendix Tables 13–16.

[2]The components do not sum to the total because of differing sample sizes.

[3]Number of countries in the SAF/ESAF sample for which data are available for a given revenue category. If the sample size varies for different columns, the maximum number is given.

changed tax revenue ratios of 20.8 percent of GDP. This last group had an average total revenue-to-GDP ratio of about 25 percent in the preprogram year. Variations in revenue targets also reflected regional differences (Appendix Table 20). In CFA franc zone countries, only a slight change in the revenue ratio was envisaged for the average program target, when compared with the preprogram year. However, this result was associated with a fall in the end-of-period revenue ratio, reflecting the steady erosion of the effective tax base over the program years owing to the progressive overvaluation of the CFA franc and the decline in real incomes immediately following the 1994 devaluation. The decline is even more pronounced when it is recognized that many CFA franc zone countries were experiencing falls in output over much of the period. (The CFA franc was subsequently devalued in January 1994.) In contrast, in non-CFA franc zone African countries, significant gains of 2.6 percent of GDP in total revenue and 1.8 percent of GDP in tax revenue were programmed. Revenue objectives in the transition economies were established in the face of significant declines in revenue mobilization, which typically accompanied the collapse of centrally planned systems. Accordingly, while the targets for these countries, on average, envisaged an increase in total-revenue-to-GDP ratios (GDP itself was also typically declining), these targets were still below the average revenue ratios that had prevailed in the three years prior to the program. Programs in Western Hemisphere and Asian countries envisaged a modest increase in the average total revenue ratio.

With regard to the components of revenue, taxes on domestic goods and services were targeted to increase by 0.8 percent of GDP over the program period.[15] Slightly more than half of the SAF/ESAF countries projected an increase in revenue from this source, often reflecting the introduction, or substantial reform, of broadly based consumption taxes such as the VAT. Taxes on income, profits, and capital gains were projected to increase slightly as a share of GDP under the programs. The share of revenue from international trade taxes was envisaged to increase by an average of 1.0 percent of GDP relative to preprogram-year ratios. Although three-fourths of the SAF/ESAF countries projected an increase in revenue from taxes on international trade, in most cases the increase was slight. As already noted, the increase can be attributed at least in part to several aspects of trade liberalization, such as the tariffication of quotas and elimination of exemptions, although, in the long term, tax reforms may be expected to reduce reliance on trade taxes relative to domestic revenue sources. In addition, the January 1994 devaluation of the CFA franc (discussed in greater detail below) was a significant factor behind envisaged increases in trade tax receipts in the CFA franc zone.[16] In some cases, however, the need for immediate revenue tended to outweigh longer-term considerations of tax reform.

---

[15]Not all countries had program targets for the components of revenue, with the result that the sample size varies.

[16]Import values in all CFA franc zone countries increased by an average of 77 percent after the devaluation.

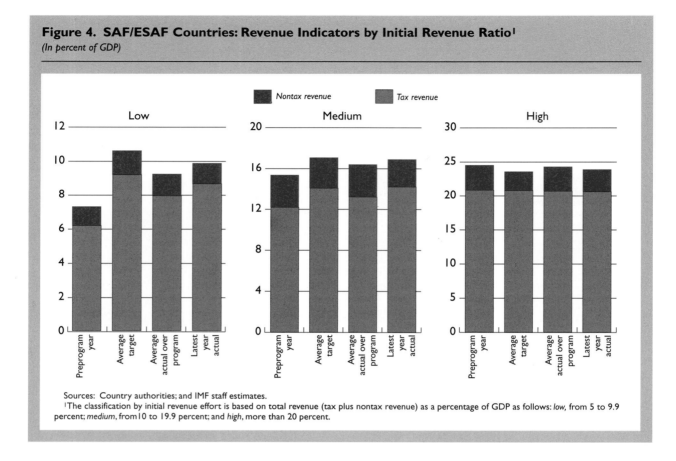

Figure 4. SAF/ESAF Countries: Revenue Indicators by Initial Revenue Ratio[1]
(In percent of GDP)

Sources: Country authorities; and IMF staff estimates.
[1]The classification by initial revenue effort is based on total revenue (tax plus nontax revenue) as a percentage of GDP as follows: *low,* from 5 to 9.9 percent; *medium,* from 10 to 19.9 percent; and *high,* more than 20 percent.

Although structural performance criteria for administrative reform measures are not widely used in SAF/ESAF programs, some did contain either prior actions or program benchmarks in the areas of tax policy and administration. Focusing on the case studies, structural benchmarks were, for instance, an important component of the programs in Benin. These benchmarks included expanding the base of the VAT laterally to a greater range of activities and downstream to the retail level, introducing controls on exemptions applicable to foreign-financed projects, adopting a simplified minimum tax on small businesses, and introducing a rationalized and simplified structure of customs duties. In Bolivia the ESAF arrangements included structural benchmarks in a range of tax and customs administration areas for every year from 1988 to 1995 with the intention of thoroughly modernizing the tax system. In Uganda the second ESAF arrangement included structural benchmarks for the preparation and adoption of the VAT law and, in the area of tax administration, for improvements in the registration of taxpayers. The programs in Albania included benchmarks on a customs administration reform program and, supported by IMF technical assistance,

the placement of customs administration advisors and the reform of customs duties.

Program Implementation

Performance vis-à-vis Annual Targets

Total revenue collected during SAF/ESAF arrangements fell short of program targets by an annual average of about 0.5 percent of GDP, with two-thirds of the countries falling below annual targets, on average, over program periods (Table 3 and Figure 5). Decomposing total revenue, *tax revenue* collections during program years were also below annual targets by 0.6 percent of GDP, on average, with 26 countries below target (of which 9 were below target by more than 1.5 percent of GDP) and only 8 above (of which 2 were above target by more than 1.5 percent of GDP). The preponderance of below-target outcomes is reflected in the fact that the corresponding median annual deviation was 1.7 percent of GDP. *Nontax revenue* exceeded program targets by an average 0.4 percent of GDP, above target in 25 countries (of which 3 were above target by more than 1.5 percent of GDP) and

Table 3. Revenue: Summary of Program Implementation
(Averages of SAF/ESAF country samples)

	Average Program Target	Average Actual During Program	Average Program Actual Minus Target[1]	Actual ≥ Target	Actual < Target	Number of Countries[2]	Pre-program Year	Latest Year[3]	Latest Year Minus Preprogram Year
	←——— In percent of GDP ———→			Percent of countries			←——— In percent of GDP ———→		
Total revenue	18.8	18.2	−0.5	33.3	66.7	36	17.1	18.1	1.0
Tax revenue	15.5	14.9	−0.6	23.5	76.5	34	14.1	15.4	1.4
Of which:									
Taxes on domestic goods and services	5.7	5.7	−0.1	34.8	65.2	23	4.9	5.6	0.6
Taxes on income, profits, and capital gains	4.6	5.3	0.7	73.9	26.1	23	4.4	4.5	0.1
Taxes on international trade	5.7	5.0	−0.7	13.0	87.0	23	4.7	4.9	0.2
Nontax revenue	2.7	3.1	0.4	73.5	26.5	34	3.0	2.7	−0.4

Sources: Country authorities; and IMF staff estimates.

[1]The components do not sum to the total because of differing sample sizes.

[2]Number of countries in the SAF/ESAF sample for which data are available for a given revenue category. If the sample size varies for different columns, the maximum number is given.

[3]Latest year for which data are available.

below in only 9 (1 of which was below target by more than 1.5 percent of GDP).[17]

There was considerable regional variation in the outcomes (Appendix Table 21). SAF/ESAF countries in Africa and Asia had significant average shortfalls in meeting total revenue targets; in contrast, Western Hemisphere and transition countries in the sample had an overall revenue performance broadly in line with program objectives. In the latter group, however, the average performance conceals an exceptionally diverse pattern, with significant "overperformance" in Albania because of the yield of near-term measures (particularly as regards nontax revenue) and Mongolia (attributable in part to favorable external developments) being balanced by "underperformance" in the Kyrgyz Republic.[18] Within the African grouping, the overall revenue objectives were, on average, broadly achieved in the CFA franc zone. However, as already noted, that performance has to be seen against the background that, for many of these countries, revised revenue targets reflected the experience of falling revenue ratios (Figure 6). Consequently, for the group as a

whole, the revenue ratio declined by an average of almost 2 percentage points of GDP between the preprogram year and the most recent year for which data are available. In addition, program performance immediately following the 1994 devaluation was disappointing—the unweighted average shortfall was about 1.3 percentage points of GDP. This weak revenue performance reflected, among other things, a larger-than-expected decline in domestic demand and a shift in consumption toward nontaxed or lower-taxed goods that was only partially compensated for by increases in revenue from taxes on trade due to the devaluation of the CFA franc in January 1994.[19] Other factors included continued problems with tax administration, including weaknesses and fraud in customs, and the continued widespread granting of exemptions, contrary to program undertakings.[20]

In the non-CFA franc zone African countries, in contrast, total revenue fell significantly short of objectives, although the revenue-to-GDP ratio increased by about 1.7 percentage points during the

---

[17]Note that the components do not sum to the total, reflecting the fact that the sample size for the components is typically smaller than that for the totals.

[18]Evidence from non-SAF/ESAF transition economies suggests that significant revenue declines are in prospect as their transition to a market economy proceeds.

[19]The value of the CFA franc was reduced from CFAF 50 to CFAF 100 per French franc (see Clément and others, 1996).

[20]Clément and others (1996), p 15. More recent data suggest that revenue performance has improved in the CFA franc zone countries in the sample, as the effect on real incomes of the 1994 devaluation has subsided, and cocoa prices have improved. On the last factor, Côte d'Ivoire reintroduced an export tax on cocoa, which has yielded significant revenue.

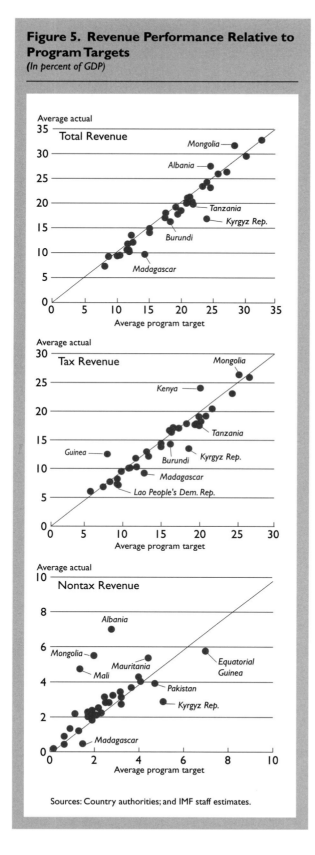

Figure 5. Revenue Performance Relative to Program Targets
(In percent of GDP)

Sources: Country authorities; and IMF staff estimates.

program period, an upward trend that is also captured in Figure 6. This shortfall relative to targets in many cases reflects a combination of relatively ambitious revenue objectives and delays in making tax policy and administrative improvements (e.g., Burundi, Madagascar, and Tanzania). The case study countries provide some further indication of the experience in this region. In Kenya, initial revenue collections from the newly introduced VAT and presumptive tax on agriculture fell short of projections because of weak administration of the VAT and overestimation of revenue from the presumptive agriculture tax. As a consequence, annual targets were revised downward. Revenue performance in Uganda was below target in part because of delays in implementing tax administration reforms and of unfavorable external developments in the coffee market.

Initial Revenue Ratio and Revenue Targets

Improvements in revenue performance relative to annual targets varied with the initial revenue levels of countries (Appendix Table 22). Countries with a high initial revenue ratio were able to exceed program targets (e.g., Lesotho and Malawi), while countries with a low or medium initial revenue ratio were unable to meet program targets (e.g., Bangladesh, Ghana, Madagascar, and Uganda). Although this may reflect in part the relatively larger revenue increases projected for the low initial revenue countries, the underperformance in these countries may also be due to the relative underdevelopment of the tax systems and administrations. For example, in the case of taxes on goods and services, countries with high initial revenue levels were able to exceed their targets by an average 0.3 percent of GDP, while low initial revenue level countries fell short of such targets by 0.4 percent of GDP. This outcome is at least in part attributable to differences in administrative capacity and in the level of development of the tax systems of each of the subgroups. By the end of 1995, only one of the low initial revenue countries (Bangladesh) had implemented a VAT while over half of the medium and high initial revenue countries had adopted a VAT. When the experience of the same countries is viewed over time, however, countries with low and medium initial revenue ratios were able to increase their actual revenue ratios significantly, suggesting that progress can be made, albeit less rapidly than sometimes envisaged, when targets are set.

Program Performance vis-à-vis Initial Three-Year Targets

ESAF programs typically incorporated initial three-year revenue targets, which were then revised

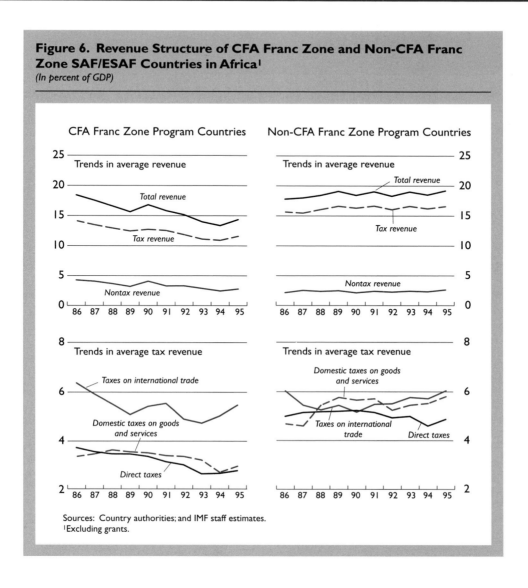

Figure 6. Revenue Structure of CFA Franc Zone and Non-CFA Franc Zone SAF/ESAF Countries in Africa[1]
(In percent of GDP)

Sources: Country authorities; and IMF staff estimates.
[1]Excluding grants.

for each annual program. For the six countries in the case studies, the initial three-year targets were compared with the revised annual targets. Of these countries, three had their annual targets revised downward from their initial three-year targets (Albania, Kenya, and Uganda), and one upward (Mongolia), while two had no significant revisions (Bolivia and Benin). Targets were revised downward for several reasons, including ambitious initial expectations of revenue gains from tax reforms—both overestimation of revenue and overoptimism about the ability of tax and customs administrations to carry out reforms (Kenya and Uganda)—and unfavorable external developments (Albania). Upward revision of targets typically followed from significant, unanticipated favorable external developments.

The comparison of the initial three-year targets with the revised annual targets was made for the sample of 20 countries that completed their three-year programs. In this sample, the objective of the initial targets was, on average, to raise total revenue at the end of the program by 1.7 percent of GDP over the revenue ratio in the preprogram year, while the revised annual targets sought a marginally smaller increase of 1.4 percent of GDP. However, for tax revenue, the initial targets aimed for a 2.4 percent of GDP increase, while the revised annual targets indicated an increase of 1.6 percent. Accordingly, revenue performance relative to initial program objectives is generally weaker than performance measured against the annual targets, although the differences at this level of aggregation do not alter the basic conclusion. With regard to nontax revenue, for which programs sought a decline in the revenue-to-GDP ratio, the initial three-year program targets were more modest, at 0.3 percent of GDP, than the revised annual targets at 0.5 percent.[21]

Revenue Components and Program Targets

Nontax revenue exceeded program targets and the case studies suggest that some countries relied on various once-off nontax measures to raise revenue, sometimes to compensate for underachievement in the area of tax reform. Albania, for example, relied on central bank transfers as well as on income from budgetary institutions and from counterpart sales of commodity aid, thereby enabling that country to exceed its revenue target. Kenya relied on increased collection of tax arrears from several of the largest parastatal enterprises as well as on profit transfers from the central bank to meet deficit targets. In these cases, increases in the revenue ratio did not signal a movement to a sounder system of revenue mobilization. In other cases, and of less concern, higher nontax revenue reflected favorable external developments. In Mongolia, nontax revenue exceeded expectations because of higher dividend payments from the state copper and cashmere enterprises based on profits derived from better-than-expected terms of trade.

SAF/ESAF countries, on average, met targets for taxes on goods and services, reflecting reasonable estimates of the impact of tax reforms. Furthermore, some of the developments noted above in the discussion of total revenue are mirrored to some degree in developments at the level of taxes on goods and services. In particular, the CFA franc zone countries satisfied the target, on average, although the contribution of sales taxes to total revenue declined significantly (by 1.3 percent of GDP) during the period between the preprogram year and the latest year for which data are available. Similarly, the non-CFA franc zone African countries, which also attained the targets for sales taxation, were able to achieve significant increases in the contribution of these taxes. (The sample sizes for the remaining regions are too small to support useful generalizations.)

Revenue from direct taxes in SAF/ESAF countries exceeded targets, on average, by 0.7 percent of GDP, in part reflecting tax policy and tax administration reforms but also reluctance to adjust personal income tax brackets in the face of inflation. These reforms have contributed to a modest increase in the GDP share of income taxes, with increases in most regions being balanced by declines in the African region. Only in some of the transition countries, as the process of economic liberalization gained momentum, did the decline in profits tax receipts from the hard-pressed state enterprise sector serve to induce a shortfall in direct tax revenue (Albania). While the data cannot be decomposed into personal and corporate components, experience has shown that gains from administrative reforms of business profit taxes, such as introducing self-assessment, creating large-taxpayer units administered by the more qualified personnel, and implementing a system of advance payments on profits tax, can improve tax receipts (Benin, Bolivia, Kenya, Mongolia, and Togo). Administrative reforms have also been found to improve revenue collections from taxes on personal income, especially where a system of withholding on wages and salaries is applied.

Insofar as the objective was to require taxes on international trade to make a significant revenue contribution, the program targets were missed in most countries, the average shortfall being 0.7 percent of GDP. Indications are that the reason for the systematic underperformance of taxes on international trade was the asymmetric implementation of reforms. The tariff rate reductions, which in many cases were implemented quickly, were not offset by the elimination of import duty exemptions or reduction of evasion, which proved to be more difficult than expected (Kenya, CFA franc zone countries, Mozambique, and Tanzania).[22] In CFA franc zone countries the overestimation of short-term revenue gains of the 1994 devaluation in taxes on international trade also played a role. In other cases, there were delays in the conversion of nontariff trade barriers into tariffs, such as in the case of countries in sub-Saharan Africa. Over one-third of all sub-Saharan African imports continue to be subject to some form of nontariff restrictions, which is more than nine times the OECD average.[23] Some countries experienced a shortfall in international trade tax receipts owing to unanticipated external developments that reduced reexport trade (The Gambia and Togo) or export prices (cocoa, in West Africa). A contributing factor was the overly ambitious targets, perhaps because of the perceived ease with which taxes (e.g., surcharges or selective increases in excises) could be imposed on imports. For instance, Côte d'Ivoire reintroduced a temporary export tax to offset losses from tariff and VAT rate reductions. Mozambique, which was recovering from war, projected higher collections in trade taxes. Finally, the data do not always permit a clean separation of customs tariffs per

---

[21]The samples for comparison of tax and nontax revenue targets were reduced to 18 and 17 countries, respectively, because of lack of data.

[22]See also Clément and others (1996).
[23]See Amjadi and others (1996).

se from other indirect taxes collected at customs, such as excises and sales taxes (Benin, Burkina Faso, Mali, Nepal, Tanzania, and Vietnam).[24] The targets for three countries projected increases in excess of 2 percent of GDP over the program period (Côte d'Ivoire, Mongolia, and Sierra Leone), while three countries projected increases in excess of 4 percent of GDP (Lesotho, Mozambique, and Tanzania). Despite missing their annual targets, these six countries nevertheless increased revenue from taxes on international trade, on average, by 3.2 percent of GDP from preprogram-year levels.

One cannot draw strong conclusions from the case studies on the effectiveness of structural benchmarks on the performance relative to targets for the three broad categories of tax revenue. However, the case studies point to a correlation between the inclusion of structural benchmarks on the reform of tariff structures and customs administration and the performance relative to targets.[25] Programs that contained explicit benchmarks or prior actions on customs reform performed better than programs that did not. While these countries also missed their respective targets, the average margin relative to the program targets is only 0.2 percent of GDP, considerably less than the sample average of 0.6 percent of GDP. Similar conclusions for taxes on goods and services and direct taxes cannot be drawn, because of insufficient information.

Changes in Tax Structure

Revenue efforts should be assessed in terms of the objective of improving the underlying structure of the tax system, to place the public finances on a permanently sound basis. Theoretically, an improved tax structure would reduce the deadweight loss associated with raising a given amount of revenue. Because this outcome is unobservable in the data used here, improvements in tax structure were approximated by comparing the relative shares of different sources of revenue before and after ESAF programs. At this level of aggregation, reductions in the relative share of nontax revenue and increases in the relative share of taxes on consumption could be taken as evidence of an improvement in the tax system. This would be on the grounds that nontax revenue sources are often arbitrary and inefficient, and the taxation of consumption is perceived to be less dis-

tortionary to resource allocation relative to all other sources of revenue. Changes in the structure of tax revenue during ESAF programs (Table 3) indicate an improvement in the average tax structure, with tax revenue rising by 1.4 percent of GDP (about one-half of which could be ascribed to an increased role for taxes on domestic goods and services), and nontax revenue falling by 0.4 percent of GDP. On a regional basis, consistent with the other findings in the paper, non-African countries improved their revenue structure slightly by this criterion,[26] whereas the revenue structure of African countries showed increases in the shares of taxes on trade. In the case of CFA franc zone countries, this increase in the relative share in taxes on trade can primarily be attributed to the transitional impact of the devaluation of the CFA franc by 50 percent in January 1994. The devaluation sharply increased the local currency value of imports and, hence, revenue from trade taxes. The increase in the ratio of trade tax revenue to GDP reflects the relatively faster response of import values to the devaluation as compared with the slower (and smaller) adjustment in the local currency value of nontradables and, more generally, GDP. At the same time, the devaluation and associated adjustment measures had the immediate effect of depressing real incomes because of the inability of households to shift away from imported goods in the short run, which in turn caused a decline in revenue from taxes on domestic consumption.

While bearing more on the issue of the appropriate size of government rather than on the structure of taxes per se, it is interesting to note that there has been some convergence in overall revenue-to-GDP ratios. Countries with low initial revenue ratios were able to achieve an increase in revenue of 2.6 percent of GDP from the preprogram year to the latest year for which data are available. The comparable increase for the medium initial revenue effort countries was 1.5 percent, while for the high initial revenue effort countries the change was a decrease of 0.6 percent of GDP.

Improvements in the structure of tax systems leading to a reduction in their distortionary effects may not immediately be reflected in large changes in the scale of revenue mobilization. However, over the medium term, the enhanced buoyancy of the more broadly based tax system, typically associated with

---

[24]In addition, some CFA franc zone countries levy special charges on reexports (primarily to Nigeria), which cannot be distinguished from standard export taxes (Benin, Togo, Niger, Mali, and Côte d'Ivoire).

[25]The reference is to structural benchmarks that were adopted in programs for Albania, Benin, Bolivia, and Uganda.

[26]Comparing the preprogram year with the most recent year for which data are available, the share of taxes on goods and services increased as follows: in Asian countries, from 34 percent to 35 percent; in transition economies, from 41 percent to 47 percent; and in Western Hemisphere countries, from 44 percent to 46 percent. In Asian and Western Hemisphere countries, taxes on trade decreased by the equivalent percentage points; in transition economies, the share of income taxes declined.

reform, should improve its revenue performance as well.

The case studies underline the central role of comprehensive tax reform in improving tax structures. Bolivia initiated fundamental reforms of the tax system and its administration in the mid-1980s, and these reforms continued under the SAF and ESAF adjustment programs adopted subsequently. Initial tax policy reforms focused on introducing a single-rate VAT and a minimum tax on businesses, while later reforms focused on simplifying and rationalizing the tariff structure. Administrative improvements included implementation of effective collection methods, establishment of large-taxpayer units, and introduction of modern audit procedures. These reforms very likely contributed to an increase in revenue effort equivalent to 3 percent of GDP relative to the preprogram year. In Uganda, an increase in total revenue of 6 percent of GDP was achieved as a result of, among other things, a broadening of the base for sales taxation and in spite of the elimination of the coffee export tax, which had accounted for more than 2 percent of GDP.

An important question in this regard is whether SAF/ESAF countries achieved, as intended, revenue mobilization through reforms that entailed reductions in statutory tax and tariff rates combined with broadening of the tax bases. Although available information does not allow for firm generalizations, detailed consideration of a sample of SAF/ESAF countries suggests that progress has been made in this regard (Box 4). Bolivia, Benin, and Uganda increased receipts from customs duties as a share of GDP over the program period, despite reductions in tariff rates (there was a modest decline in such revenue in the case of Kenya). Moreover, as with customs collections, these countries also increased tax revenue as a share of GDP, despite reductions in marginal tax rates.

While contrary examples have already been cited, a number of countries reduced their reliance on *non-tax revenue* over the program periods. Indeed, a fundamental focus of reform in the transition economies (e.g., the Kyrgyz Republic) has been to shift from reliance on extracting surpluses from state enterprises to reliance on market-oriented, buoyant sources of taxation. In the Western Hemisphere, Bolivia's increase in total revenue relative to its preprogram year was the net result of an increase of 15.6 percentage points of GDP in tax revenue (from an exceptionally low initial level) and decline of 12.6 percentage points of GDP in nontax receipts. Although CFA franc countries as a group had an average decline in both tax and nontax revenue, an exception is Benin, which showed an improvement in tax collection and reduced reliance on nontax receipts. Burkina Faso's experience broadly parallels that of Benin.

Turning to the components of tax revenue, we found the most comprehensive tax reforms focused on taxes on domestic goods and services, notably through the introduction of new, broad-based taxes on domestic consumption, such as the VAT (Box 5). The CFA franc zone witnessed significant reform in this area with the completion of VAT implementation in the countries of the West African region of the CFA franc zone.[27] VATs have also been relied upon in the transition and Latin American economies. Indeed, by September 1995, 16 SAF/ESAF countries had implemented a VAT. Moreover, during the sample period the standard statutory rate of these taxes tended to converge to between 15 percent and 20 percent, that is, within the range that the IMF typically recommends for introduction of the VAT.[28]

However, the contribution of a *new VAT* to structural reform and revenue mobilization depends critically on the details of the tax and the strength of tax administration. Consider the examples of Bangladesh, Benin, and Burkina Faso, three countries whose VATs most closely conform with the model characterized in Box 5. For these three countries, the (unweighted) GDP share of taxes on domestic goods and services rose from an average of 0.65 percent in the year before VAT implementation to an average 1.9 percent in 1995 (over an average period of about three years). Although difficult to compare with the prior sales tax regime, the VAT implemented in Bolivia attests to the buoyancy of a well-structured and administered tax—the yield rose from an average of 2.5 percent of GDP during 1987–88 to an average of 5.8 percent of GDP during 1994–95.

Expansion of the VAT base and improvements in administration also helped to improve revenue buoyancy. For example, expansion of the VAT to the retail sector in Kenya led to better-than-expected revenue outturns, though other changes were less desirable. Following its introduction in Bolivia, the VAT was expanded, which contributed substantially to the sharp increase in revenue already noted. In Benin and Bolivia the VAT served as a catalyst for introducing modern systems and procedures for tax and customs administration while providing a buoyant source of revenue.

For the sample as a whole, however, experience with the VAT has been quite varied, as some of the VATs have been implemented with, or have acquired, undesirable features. These departures from "best practices" VAT structures have produced a

---

[27]Côte d'Ivoire and Senegal introduced VATs in 1960 and 1961, respectively, while Equatorial Guinea has yet to introduce a VAT. The other five countries (Benin, Burkina Faso, Mali, Niger, and Togo) introduced VATs during 1986 to 1995 (Box 5).

[28]From 1989 to 1995, two countries (Kenya and Malawi) lowered their statutory standard VAT rates, while three others (Bolivia, Honduras, and Nicaragua) increased theirs.

Box 4. Lowering Marginal Tax Rates

While supporting fiscal consolidation through revenue mobilization was a focus of many SAF/ESAF-supported programs, those programs also typically stressed reforms that contributed to the efficiency and fairness of tax systems. A useful rough indicator of progress in this respect is the degree to which high and variable (marginal) tax rates are reduced or rationalized. The following cases afford some examples of the progress that has been made.

Bangladesh: The top marginal personal income tax rate was reduced to 25 percent in 1994 from 50 percent in 1985. During the same period, the corporate income tax rate was decreased to 50 percent from 60 percent. The revenue effects were positive: both tax revenue as a percentage of GDP and the share of income taxes in tax revenue increased. Customs tariffs in Bangladesh were reduced to 0–60 percent from 0–300 percent, while reducing the number of exemptions.

Benin: In 1990 the standard corporate tax rate was reduced to 38 percent from 48 percent over the program period while at the same time the equivalent rate on individual enterprises was raised to a level closer to the standard corporate rate. As part of trade liberalization, the tariff structure was simplified and rationalized by reducing the number of tariffs to four and lowering the top statutory tariff rate to 20 percent from 90 percent in 1994.

Bolivia: The objectives of tax reform included introducing a broad-based tax on domestic consumption in the form of a VAT and the liberalization of the structure of international trade taxes. Accordingly, in March 1988 the tariff structure was simplified with the adoption of a 10 percent rate for capital imports and an initial rate of 19 percent for other imports that was gradually reduced to 5 percent on capital imports and 10 percent on other imports in 1994. This reduction was supported by structural performance criteria. Notwithstanding the tariff reductions, the effective tariff rate remained unchanged, partly as the result of a reduction in exemptions.

Kenya: There were a number of tax rate reductions and rationalizations in the Kenyan tax system. The top marginal personal income tax rate was reduced to 35 percent from 65 percent in 1995, along with a broadening of income tax brackets. At the same time the base was broadened by introducing withholding on income from financial instruments and making the full value of employee benefits subject to tax. Also at the same time, the corporate income tax rate for resident companies was reduced to 35 percent from 45 percent and various investment incentives were eliminated. As regards international trade taxes, the maximum import duty rate was cut to 40 percent in the 1990/91 budget year from 125 percent, with a reduction in the number of items in the top band. This reduced not only the level but also the dispersion of rates. Export duties were eliminated. During the program period the VAT rate structure was changed from five to three rates. In addition, the VAT base was expanded to cover over 80 percent of the retail sector and services.

Uganda: Authorities cut the top marginal personal income tax rate from 60 percent in 1989 to 30 percent in 1993, while broadening the tax base through the inclusion of, among other categories, rental income, allowances, and benefits. Concurrently, the corporate income tax rate was reduced to 30 percent, the same rate as the top personal income tax rate. This was combined with a streamlining of investment incentives. Import tariffs also were rationalized, with a reduction in the number of tariff bands to four from six and a compression of the tariff band to 0–30 percent from 0–50 percent.

As shown in Appendix Tables 14 and 17, even as these significant reductions in statutory tax rates were implemented, tax revenue expressed as a percentage of GDP increased in all cases when comparing revenue in the preprogram year with the latest data available. Revenue from international trade taxes by this measure also increased, with the exception of Kenya (modest decline) and Bangladesh (broadly unchanged).

---

mixed picture with regard to the efficiency of the tax systems and the buoyancy of revenue performance in the sample as a whole. Indeed, the overall impact of the VAT experience in SAF/ESAF countries is, at this level of aggregation, ambiguous because of this diversity and the difficulties of assessing the "quality" of a particular VAT from available data. For example, of those countries that had a VAT at the beginning of their SAF/ESAF program, two countries improved the structure of their VATs by reducing the number of statutory rates (Côte d'Ivoire and Senegal). In contrast, Nicaragua undertook to reform the VAT but only increased its complexity by raising the number of statutory rates. Turning to those cases where VATs were implemented during the program periods, we found three of the VATs departed significantly from standard international practice by limiting credits on taxes paid on inputs thereby introducing an element of tax cascading (Malawi, Mongolia, and Pakistan). In other cases the VAT was implemented with rates in excess of the range of 15–20 percent, and with multiple rates that created distortions in relative prices and increased compliance and administration costs (Kenya and Malawi). After the introduction, however, some countries did simplify the VAT by reducing the number of rates (Kenya and Malawi).

Finally, and in conjunction with general sales tax reform, many countries reformed *excise taxes*. Some countries raised excise rates on selected goods and services (Kenya and Uganda) or converted excises from specific to ad valorem rates (Benin, Burundi, Ghana, Guyana, Kenya, Malawi, Mauritania, Mongolia, Tanzania, and Uganda).

Box 5. Why the VAT?

The introduction of the VAT has been among the most significant tax reforms carried out during the past two decades in many developing countries and transition economies—as well as in some industrialized countries. In a number of SAF/ESAF countries, the VAT has also been at the center of the tax policy and tax administration reform efforts.

Within the sample of 36 SAF/ESAF countries, 16 had a VAT by the end of 1995 and 5 more either introduced it during 1996 or have scheduled its introduction for the immediate future (see VAT table). In many of these countries, the introduction or reform of the VAT accompanied the repeal of multiple levies with low yields (e.g., Bolivia) and often replaced taxes on turnover (e.g., Benin, Kenya, Kyrgyz Republic, Mongolia, and Uganda) that had caused "cascading," which distorts prices, artificially favors imports and vertical integration, and hinders export industries. Such taxes are also difficult to administer.

In contrast the VAT offers several advantages. First, the revenue-raising potential of the VAT, even at moderately low rates, has proven to be substantial, even for countries in the early stages of economic development. Second, as the tax burden of the VAT falls mainly on consumption, it minimizes the disincentives to save and invest, which are often present in other taxes. Third, provided that it has a broad base with few exemptions and a single rate (or at least the rate dispersion is minimal), the VAT does not alter the relative prices of alternative consumption goods and services and, therefore, minimizes tax-induced obstacles to the efficient allocation of resources. Finally, as a result of the inclusion of imports in the tax base, the credit mechanism, and the zero-rating of export activities, the VAT is an effective tool in insulating a country's international competitiveness from its domestic tax burden.

The IMF typically recommends that countries adopt a VAT with a single rate in the range of 15 percent to 20 percent, few exemptions, zero-rating only for exports, and crediting for all inputs. Because the VAT is often implemented as a replacement for existing taxes on goods and services, its introduction is often planned as revenue neutral, to help reduce initial opposition. The IMF generally recommends that excises be reformed at the time the VAT is introduced, with a view to converting specific rates to ad valorem rates and eliminating unproductive excises.

Contrary to initial fears, it became evident during the 1970s that with proper planning and adequate administrative resources, the VAT could be successfully introduced in economies at various degrees of development. Countries that enacted VATs often made this tax the focus of tax administration reform (e.g., Benin, Bolivia, and Togo) by, for example, creating special units to deal with large taxpayers (which generally account for a disproportionately high ratio of total revenue), by computerizing, and by improving audits. The enhanced administrative efficiency that followed had positive effects on compliance with other taxes (e.g., corporate income taxes), because of the improved exploitation of taxpayer databases.

A number of countries also undertook important *direct taxation reforms* beyond the reductions in top marginal rates already noted. These reforms aimed, among other things, at broadening the tax bases by reducing exemptions and deductions (Benin and Uganda) and shifting from schedular to global income taxes (Bolivia, Guyana, Madagascar, Malawi, Pakistan, and Tanzania). Business profits tax reforms sought to improve tax collection, in part, through a reform of the system of incentives for new investment (Uganda); by levying advance tax payments on a periodic and current basis (Kenya and Malawi); by instituting simplified tax regimes for small enterprises and the informal sector (Benin and Togo); and by introducing presumptive taxes on turnover or assets of corporations (Bolivia).

Although most SAF/ESAF countries underperformed relative to program targets on revenue from international trade taxes, they showed an average increase of approximately 0.2 percent of GDP between the preprogram year and the most recent year for which data are available (Table 2). Improved yields or revenue shortfalls in this regard may be related to the success or failure of tariff and customs reforms or changes in trade volumes; the relative importance of either factor is not always easy to determine. Nevertheless, in some countries, the strengthening of customs administration and policy reform contributed to increases in customs revenue of, on average, about 1.5 percent of GDP over program periods (Burkina Faso, Bolivia, and Uganda). A number of countries also reduced the adverse allocational impact of trade taxes by reducing or eliminating export duties on primary products. For example, a significant achievement of tax reform in Uganda was the elimination of the coffee export tax and, in Kenya, the elimination of export taxes on commodities and manufactured products. In a few countries, however, export duties were reintroduced or maintained as a proxy for an income tax in hard-to-tax agriculture (e.g., Côte d'Ivoire and Ghana).

VAT: Dates of Introduction and Rate Structure

Country	Program Years or Years Covered	Year of Introduction (or projected)	Rate(s) at Introduction[1]	Rate(s) in September 1995[1]
Africa				
CFA franc countries				
Benin	1989–91, 1993–95	1991	18	18
Burkina Faso	1991, 1993–95	1993	10, **15**	**15**
Côte d'Ivoire	1994–95	1960	8	**11**, 20
Mali	1988–90, 1992–95	1991	10, **17**	**10**, 15
Niger	1986–88, 1990	1986	8, 12, **18**	**17**
Senegal	1986–91, 1994–95	1961–80	2	**10**, 20
Togo	1988–90, 1994	1995	7, **18**	...
Non-CFA franc countries				
Ghana	1987–92, 1995	3	...	...
Kenya	1987/88–91/92, 1993/94–94/95	1990	**17**, 20, 40, 50, 270	6, **15**, 25
Malawi[4]	1988/89–93/94, 1995/96	1989	10, **35**, 55, 85	10, **20**, 40
Asia				
Bangladesh	1986/87–88/89, 1990/91–92/93	1991	**15**	**15**
Pakistan[4]	1988/89–89/90, 1991/92, 1993/94–94/95	1990	**12.5**	10, 12.5, **15**, 17, 20
Western Hemisphere				
Bolivia	1987–92, 1994–95	1973	5, 10, **15**	**14.92**
Honduras	1992–93, 1995	1976	3	**7**, 10
Nicaragua	1994	1975	6	5, 6, 10, **15**
Transition economies				
Kyrgyz Republic	1994–95	1992	**28**	**20**
Mongolia[4]	1993–95	1993	**10**	**10**

Source: IMF staff.

[1]Rates shown in bold type are so-called effective standard rates (tax exclusive) applied to goods and services not covered by other special rates. Most countries have an additional zero rate, which is applied mostly to exports.

[2]Senegal's VAT evolved from a limited turnover tax with credits on manufacturers. No precise date of introduction is available.

[3]The VAT was introduced on March 1, 1995, with a rate of 17.5 percent, and repealed on June 6, 1995.

[4]These VAT-type taxes do not allow full crediting for all tax paid on business inputs.

In a number of cases, the increase in revenue can be attributed mainly to immediate revenue-raising measures, including an increase in duty rates (Cambodia) and the introduction of temporary export taxes (Malawi). The underperformance of the CFA franc zone countries appears to be primarily due to an overestimation of increases in trade values in response to the 1994 devaluation.[29]

Completed versus Interrupted Programs

To this point, countries with on-time completion of SAF/ESAF programs have not been distinguished from those that experienced interruptions in completing programs. An analysis of this factor indicates that countries with no interruptions experienced increased tax revenue ratios from all sources relative to their respective preprogram years (Table 4).[30] However, to the extent that countries maintained their tax reform efforts during nonprogram periods, interruptions would not necessarily be linked to slippages in performance. In this regard, the aggregate data mask the sustained reform efforts over the SAF/ESAF period of a number of countries—for example, Benin and Ghana with two interruptions, and Bolivia with three. The performance of countries with interruptions relative to targets is virtually indistinguishable from that of countries with no interruptions.

As another proxy for program success, one could consider the extent to which a country received

[29]Increases in trade values in response to the 1994 devaluation were overestimated on average by 22 percent for this group of countries (see Clément and others, 1996). In part, this occurred because the devaluation had been widely anticipated and some evidence of overimporting before and underimporting after the devaluation was observed.

[30]There are 8 countries that had no interruptions, 10 with only one interruption, 12 with two interruptions, and 6 with three interruptions.

Table 4. Revenue: Summary of Program Implementation by Number of Program Interruptions[1]
(In percent of GDP; averages of SAF/ESAF country samples)

	Number of Interruptions				
	0	1	2	3	All countries
Change from preprogram year to latest year[2]					
Total revenue	3.0	1.4	−0.4	0.5	1.0
Tax revenue	2.6	1.4	−0.1	2.8	1.4
Of which:					
Taxes on domestic goods and services	1.2	0.4	0.4	2.7	0.7
Taxes on income, profits, and capital gains	0.4	0.3	−0.2	0.2	0.1
Taxes on international trade	0.9	0.7	−0.4	0.2	0.2
Nontax revenue	0.4	−0.1	−0.3	−1.9	−0.4
Average performance relative to program target[3]					
Total revenue	−0.6	−0.3	−0.7	−0.6	−0.5
Tax revenue	−1.4	−0.2	−0.9	0.7	−0.6
Of which:					
Taxes on domestic goods and services	0.1	—	−0.4	−0.1	−0.2
Taxes on income, profits, and capital gains	−1.0	2.4	0.5	1.6	0.7
Taxes on international trade	−0.4	−0.7	−0.5	−0.8	−0.6
Nontax revenue	0.4	0.4	0.7	−0.3	0.4

Sources: Country authorities; and IMF staff estimates.

[1]The components do not sum to the total because of differing sample sizes. A *program interruption* is defined as either an interval of more than six months between different IMF arrangements, an interval of more than six months between annual arrangements, or a delay of more than six months in completing an ESAF program review.

[2]A negative number indicates the preprogram year exceeds the latest year for which data are available.

[3]A negative number indicates target exceeds actual.

approval of three annual arrangements and completion of the three midterm reviews under the country's first ESAF-supported adjustment program. Countries that completed their first ESAF program exhibited an increase in tax revenue from all sources relative to the preprogram year. In contrast, countries that failed to complete their first ESAF programs exhibited a decline in tax revenue relative to the preprogram year. The first group of countries also achieved actual revenue ratios much closer to their targets.

Tax Administration

Reforms of tax administration have reinforced the introduction of more modern tax structures in many SAF/ESAF countries. In some countries, a first step in the reform of the tax administration was to simplify taxes, a step that was complemented by administrative reforms (Box 6). More generally, reforms of the tax administration typically included elements such as wider registration of taxpayers, the simplification of procedures for taxing the informal sector, the establishment of large-taxpayer units, and staff training and computerization. Tax administration reforms typically have long gestation lags and, therefore, cannot be uti-

lized as short-term revenue measures. For example, the introduction of a VAT in Benin was implemented over an extended period and was the catalyst for other reforms in tax administration.

Appropriate sequencing of tax reform is important for the overall success of the reform strategy, especially given the limited administrative capacity of many SAF/ESAF countries. In this connection the early focus on implementing a VAT, beyond its importance for revenue, can be justified in terms of motivating necessary improvements in overall revenue administration. Drawing on the case studies, Benin, Kenya, and, more recently, Uganda have used the introduction of new systems and procedures for the VAT as a catalyst for reforming the administration of other taxes. A successful VAT comes with a package of new administrative systems and procedures that replace existing, and often antiquated, policies and practices. These new procedures include the reforms mentioned above and, more specifically, implementing unique taxpayer identification numbers, introducing self-assessment, and developing audit plans and procedures. These reforms are often reinforced, or followed, by the introduction of new systems and procedures for taxing small businesses and the informal sector, including the introduction of presumptive

Box 6. Tax Administration Reforms

The success of revenue mobilization over the medium term depends significantly on the implementation of comprehensive reforms in tax administration. The following case studies afford examples of the scope of such reforms, including strengthening institutional capacity and improving systems and procedures. In some cases, these reforms entailed giving greater autonomy to tax administration, with promising results.

Benin: Reforms aimed at improving tax collection procedures included the widening of taxpayer registration and an increase in staff training and computerization. Moreover, the introduction of the VAT in 1991 provided a catalyst for introducing modern tax and customs administration systems and procedures, including increased coordination and cooperation between the tax and customs departments, introduction of a unique tax identification number (TIN) for all tax transactions, computerization of the taxpayer register, and creation of a large-taxpayer unit. In addition, the customs directorate improved and modernized its computer systems, strengthened inspections, introduced a preshipment inspection system, and improved controls on transit trade.

Bolivia: Tax and customs administration reforms were linked to ESAF arrangements through structural performance criteria, which included implementation of a computerized tax collection system (1988), creation of directorates to handle large taxpayers subject to VAT and consumption taxes in three major cities (1988), implementation of an action plan to reform customs administration (1989), privatization of 12 customs houses

(1992), and completion of construction of three customs houses on the border with Chile (1994).

Mongolia: Technical assistance helped facilitate the implementation of tax administration reforms, specifically through the transformation of the tax administration from a unit in the ministry of finance to a separate agency organized largely on a functional basis and through the introduction of a basic tax administration law. Technical assistance was also instrumental in the implementation of a large-taxpayer unit, the development of a national audit plan, and the preparation of an audit manual used by all auditors throughout the country. However, because of administrative capacity constraints, progress has been limited in some important areas, notably collection enforcement and computerization.

Uganda: Tax collections as a percentage of GDP grew significantly after 1992, underpinned by tax administration reforms. A key development was the institution of the Uganda Revenue Authority (URA) in 1992, resulting in improvements in customs valuations procedures and sales tax administration, including through the development of accurate taxpayer registers and effective collection procedures. In addition to improving the incentive structure and training for the development of a professional staff, the URA provided adequate accommodation, vehicles, and equipment for carrying out improved administrative procedures. From 1992 through 1994, these improvements contributed to a 1.7 percent of GDP increase in revenue collection from taxes on domestic goods and services and a 0.9 percent of GDP increase in international trade tax collections.

---

taxes on these sectors. Once the VAT system is operational, new systems and procedures for administering the tax are often then extended to other taxes such as the business income tax and withholding taxes on wages and salaries.

A significant feature of tax administration reform in many SAF/ESAF countries was the establishment of an autonomous tax administration separate from the finance ministry or treasury and, in some cases, outside the regular civil service. Separating tax administration from the regular civil service and thus providing more flexibility in setting salary levels of tax officials and in hiring and firing staff, if supported by political commitment and reinforced by organizational reforms, has been found to enhance productivity and contribute to substantial revenue gains (see the example of Uganda cited in Box 6), although there are cases in which the initial granting of autonomy was withdrawn (Ghana). Along with granting the revenue administration greater autonomy, the change often created opportunities to make organiza-

tional changes that supported implementation of more efficient, modern procedures. The Uganda example encouraged the establishment of similar revenue authorities in other African countries, such as in Kenya and, more recently, Tanzania.

As is clear from the case studies, technical assistance, when well designed and implemented in line with growth in local capacity, can play an important role in tax administration reform. Indeed, technical assistance from the IMF and other providers has proven to be a catalyst for authorities to undertake fundamental tax administration reform in a number of SAF/ESAF countries. It has focused particularly on building institutional capacity aimed at increasing voluntary compliance and self-assessment, expanding the use of final withholding, improving collection procedures, developing audit plans and procedures, and reorganizing the tax administration along functional lines, generally with positive results (Albania, Benin, Bolivia, Guinea, Mongolia, Mozambique, and Uganda).

IV Expenditure Policy and Performance

As noted above, expenditure reforms are necessary for ensuring macroeconomic stability, promoting growth, and enhancing the efficiency of public expenditures. This section discusses expenditure policy objectives underlying the SAF/ESAF-supported programs and the success in achieving these objectives.

Expenditure Objectives and Program Targets

SAF/ESAF-supported programs in their annual targets have aimed, on average, to more or less maintain total expenditure as a share of GDP while shifting expenditure from current to capital spending. In contrast, expenditure reductions were foreseen in the initial three-year targets. Budgetary savings in annual targets were anticipated from cuts in excessive public sector employment and inefficient subsidies and transfers, and capital spending, in particular on basic infrastructure and the social sectors, was to increase. Public spending would be made more efficient through improvements in budgeting and expenditure management. Further gains in expenditure productivity were incorporated in a number of programs, including through the reallocation of resources to basic health care and primary education, improvements in the targeting of basic services to the most needy, and a reduction in excessive military spending.

Spending had typically declined in the years leading up to the SAF/ESAF program, but the program itself did not, on average, seek a further decline on the basis of annual targets.[31] The program target for total spending, on average, was 28.2 percent of GDP compared with an average actual spending of 29.0 percent of GDP in the three years before the program and 27.6 percent of GDP in the preprogram year

(Table 5 and Figure 7).[32] Just under half of the countries in the sample (17 countries) targeted increases in total expenditures relative to the three-year preprogram average with a view to rehabilitating or strengthening a country's infrastructure (Bangladesh and Ghana), increasing public investment (Bolivia), or providing competitive wages for skilled public sector employees (Ghana) (Appendix Table 23). Based on a sample of 47 three-year arrangements out of a total of 68 covered in this review, expenditure targets at the time of approval envisaged a reduction in total noninterest outlays of 1.9 percent of GDP by the end of the three-year program relative to the preprogram year.[33]

African countries overall programmed a reduction of 0.3 percent of GDP relative to the three-year preprogram average. Within Africa, CFA franc zone countries targeted a large spending reduction of 2.3 percentage points of GDP. Several transition countries (Albania and Mongolia), on the other hand, targeted reductions of more than 10 percent of GDP in light of their higher preprogram spending levels and the changing role of government in their economies.

Capital spending was viewed as potentially more efficient at the margin than current spending, although some public investment has, in fact, been relatively unproductive. An average increase in capital expenditure of 1.4 percentage points of GDP and an average reduction in current expenditure of 2.2 percentage points of GDP were targeted relative to the three-year preprogram average, thus implying a significant reduction in the share of current spending in the total. All expenditure savings in CFA franc zone countries were projected from a reduction in current spending of 2.6 percentage points of GDP vis-à-vis the three-year preprogram average. For other African countries, a sharp increase in capital spending of

---

[31]The preprogram year spending in Table 5 represents actual *ex post* spending in that year, as a share of GDP. Using projected or estimated preprogram year spending at the time program targets were established would change the ratios somewhat but would not alter the results of the analysis.

[32]Program targets refer to targets set at the beginning of each annual program within the three-year SAF/ESAF arrangement, including subsequent revisions of the program targets. Although these revisions were substantial in Guyana and Senegal, they were rather marginal in the aggregate; the average program target was 0.1 percentage point of GDP higher under the original annual programs than under the revised targets.

[33]See International Monetary Fund (forthcoming).

Table 5. Expenditure: Summary of Program Targets
(Averages of SAF/ESAF country samples)

	Average of Three Years Prior to Program	Pre-program Year	Average Program Target	Target > Preprogram Average	Target < Preprogram Average	Number of Countries[1]
	←——— In percent of GDP[2] ———→			*Percent of countries*		
Total expenditure and net lending	29.0	27.6	28.2	49	51	36
Current expenditure	20.9	19.7	18.7	43	57	36
Goods and services	13.6	12.6	11.9	38	62	28
Wages and salaries	7.1	6.5	6.1	37	63	33
Other	6.3	5.8	6.0	40	60	28
Interest	4.0	3.9	4.0	71	29	35
Subsidies and transfers	4.4	3.9	3.2	40	60	29
Other	3.9	3.9	5.1	43	57	21
Capital expenditure and net lending	7.9	7.7	9.3	66	34	36
	←——— In percent of total expenditure and net lending ———→					
Total expenditure and net lending						
Current expenditure	70.5	69.6	65.4	31	69	36
Goods and services	44.4	43.4	40.5	29	71	28
Wages and salaries	24.9	23.7	22.4	37	63	33
Other	19.7	19.9	19.5	40	60	29
Interest	12.3	12.5	13.5	71	29	35
Subsidies and transfers	12.4	12.6	9.6	35	65	31
Other	16.1	15.9	17.9	38	62	20
Capital expenditure and net lending	28.9	29.7	34.0	71	29	36

Sources: Country authorities; and IMF staff estimates.

[1]Number of countries for which data are available for a given expenditure category. If the sample size varies for different columns, the maximum figure is given.

[2]The sum of the expenditure components may differ from the totals because of differences in sample size.

nearly 2 percentage points of GDP was expected to more than offset a cut in current expenditure. For transition countries, the program shift from current to capital spending was more pronounced, with current spending targeted to decline by 3 percentage points of GDP (Appendix Table 24), and capital spending targeted to rise by an equivalent amount (Appendix Table 25).

Nearly half of the savings in current spending was expected from *wages and salaries*; these were targeted to fall by an average of 1 percent of GDP. In virtually all SAF/ESAF countries, civil service reform constituted an important element of program design, with the World Bank mostly taking the lead. In general, reform aimed at some combination of reducing the excessive numbers of public sector employees, eliminating "ghost" workers, maintaining competitive wages (in particular, for high-skilled employees), eliminating distortions in the wage structure by increasing the differentials and reducing nonwage benefits, and restructuring ministries and rationalizing their functions. These were often accompanied by civil service surveys or efforts to oth-

erwise improve the personnel database and personnel management systems. Some of the expenditure savings in the short term were to be used for compensating departing government workers. However, there was considerable variation among countries regarding the programmed wage bill. For countries in Africa, the wage bill was set, on average, to decline by 1.4 percent of GDP, while for other ESAF countries, a much smaller decline (0.5 percent of GDP) was programmed (Appendix Table 26). The targeted average reduction in the wage bill in CFA franc countries was 1.8 percentage points of GDP, reflecting relatively high initial wage levels in these countries. In about one-third of the countries, wages and salaries were targeted to increase, in some cases by more than 1 percentage point of GDP (Burundi and Ghana).

Subsidies and transfers were programmed to decline by 1.2 percentage points of GDP, or about half of the programmed cut in current spending, reflecting in part lower transfers to public enterprises and a better targeting of consumer subsidies. In transition economies, where such spending played an especially large role in the preprogram period, significantly

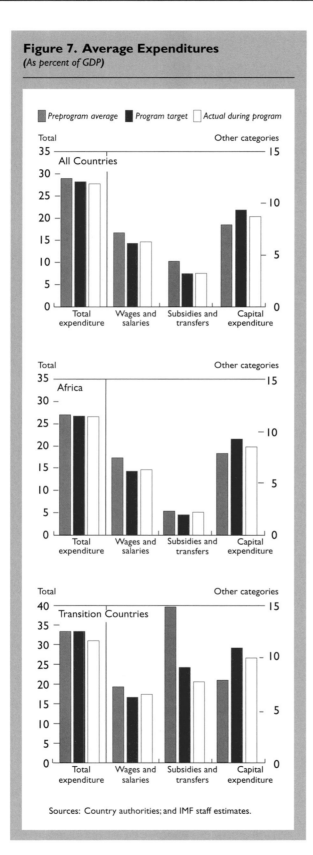

Figure 7. Average Expenditures
(As percent of GDP)

■ Preprogram average ■ Program target □ Actual during program

All Countries

Africa

Transition Countries

Sources: Country authorities; and IMF staff estimates.

larger declines were programmed (Appendix Table 27). Generalized consumer subsidies are an inefficient means of increasing the consumption of the poor, and budgetary transfers to enterprises often sustain inefficient state-owned firms. In Africa, where subsidies and transfers constituted a smaller share of GDP than for all ESAF countries, a decline of 0.4 percent of GDP was programmed. Interest payments, as a share of GDP, were programmed to remain broadly unchanged relative to the three-year preprogram average, although higher interest payments were programmed for more than 70 percent of the countries.

Other Aspects of Expenditure Policy

Other elements of expenditure policy noted in the more recent programs included calls for increased spending on basic social services and infrastructure, or for protecting such spending from cuts. Programs have sought increased real education and health spending (Côte d'Ivoire, Equatorial Guinea, Lesotho, Mozambique, and Uganda), and a larger share for the social sectors in recurrent expenditure (health for Lao People's Democratic Republic and Mali, education for Togo). In some cases, programs sought an improvement in the *intrasectoral* allocation by reallocating outlays toward basic health care and primary education (Bangladesh and Bolivia). Improvements in the efficiency and benefit incidence of expenditure were also sought through increases in user charges (e.g., for water in Pakistan, and higher education in Kenya). In recent years, programs have increasingly set quantitative targets for intrasectoral spending (primary or peripheral health in Bolivia and Malawi, and primary health and basic education in Zimbabwe). They also stressed the need to maintain adequate levels of spending for operations and maintenance (Bangladesh and Ghana) and to reduce excessive military spending (Pakistan and Zimbabwe), making room for more productive public spending on areas such as basic health care and primary education.

However, in some countries where these quantitative targets were incorporated in programs, they could not be monitored because of data problems. For example, data on social spending were sometimes inconsistent (Burundi), data coverage was partial (Uganda data covered only recurrent spending), or data were available only with a lag of two years (Togo). In one country (Lao People's Democratic Republic), targets referred only to budget allocations. For another country (Bolivia), the program sought a specific increase in the share of health spending allocated to primary health, but disaggregated data are not yet available.

Many SAF/ESAF countries attempted to incorporate temporary social safety nets and their budgetary cost to the programs, with the objective of shielding the most vulnerable during reform periods and enhancing the political viability of structural reforms. Safety nets have sought to mitigate the adverse short-term effects of price increases and reduced employment opportunities on vulnerable population groups.

Quantitative Program Targets and Benchmarks

On occasion, quantitative targets were used as benchmarks to influence expenditure outcomes. Quantitative targets for expenditure composition were included in the program for Bangladesh, which targeted an increase of 1 percentage point of GDP in capital spending and a reduction by the same amount in current spending. No such quantitative targets were set for functional categories of spending (health or education), perhaps reflecting the lack of timely data. However, indicative targets were sometimes included in policy framework papers for such spending. Benchmarks, or structural performance criteria, were set for implementing pension reform (Bolivia) or raising the pensionable age (Kyrgyz Republic), and for reducing the size of the civil service (Zimbabwe). In addition, benchmarks were set for specific measures to improve expenditure management, including the establishment of a treasury (Kyrgyz Republic), the development and implementation in key ministries of a new budget and expenditure management system (Ghana), and the consolidation of current and capital budgets within the treasury (Togo). Some recent programs have included benchmarks for federal transfers for basic social services (Pakistan) and implementation of social safety nets (Lesotho). IMF technical assistance recommendations for reform of social safety nets and pension systems and for improvement of expenditure efficiency have been incorporated as structural benchmarks (Kyrgyz Republic).

Program Implementation

Performance vis-à-vis Annual Targets

Total expenditure averaged some 0.5 percent of GDP less than programmed, and spending fell short of program targets in about half of the cases (e.g., Guyana, the Kyrgyz Republic, Lao People's Democratic Republic, and Mozambique) (Table 6 and Figure 8).[34] Lower-than-programmed spending was traceable to shortfalls in revenue and less-than-anticipated foreign funding to support the capital budget or limited capacity to implement projects. Among ESAF countries in Africa, spending in the CFA franc zone countries fell short of program, by 0.7 percent of GDP, while for non-CFA franc zone countries, actual spending slightly exceeded the programmed level.

The data suggest a relationship between shortfalls in revenue and expenditure, in particular capital expenditure. Overall, for 23 of the 36 countries (64 percent), average revenue during the program, as a share of GDP, fell short of programmed levels, while average expenditure was less than programmed in 17 countries (47 percent). Of those 23 countries with revenue shortfalls, 12 (52 percent) also experienced shortfalls in total expenditure, while capital spending was lower than programmed for 18 (78 percent). On the other hand, only 9 of the 23 countries (39 percent) with revenue shortfalls had current spending that was below programmed levels. This supports the notion that unexpected revenue shortfalls have typically led to cuts in public investment.

Over the entire period of the programs, SAF/ESAF countries reduced total spending by an average of 2.6 percentage points of GDP between the three-year preprogram period and the most recent year for which data are available, with more than half of the countries reducing spending. SAF/ESAF countries in Africa typically entered programs with lower levels of total spending as a share of GDP than other program countries, and reduced spending by less than other program countries, relative to both preprogram and programmed spending levels. The pattern, however, is different for CFA franc zone countries, which experienced greater spending reductions (by more than 4 percentage points of GDP) than other countries in Africa, reflecting their greater reliance on fiscal instruments to correct macroeconomic imbalances.

Program Performance vis-à-vis Initial Three-Year Targets

In the six countries for which initial targets were analyzed, four overspent and two underspent in relation to these targets.[35] Actual spending levels and patterns appear to have diverged further from original program targets than from annual targets. This is not surprising, as annual targets reflect external developments, as well as revised staff judgments regarding, for example, revenue developments, project implementation capacity or the availability of foreign financing, and the ability of the country to

---

[34]The average number of annual programs for each country in the sample was five.

[35]The comparison for Bolivia cited here refers to performance vis-à-vis original SAF targets for 1987–89, and ESAF targets in Bangladesh are from 1990–92.

Table 6. Expenditure: Summary of Program Implementation
(Averages of SAF/ESAF country samples)

	Average Program Target	Average Actual During Program	Average Program Actual Minus Target[1]	Latest Year Available[2]	Actual> Target	Actual< Target	Number of Countries[3]
	← In percent of GDP →				Percent of countries		
Total expenditure and net lending	28.2	27.7	−0.5	26.2	47	53	36
Current expenditure	18.7	18.8	—	17.9	53	47	36
Goods and services	11.9	12.1	0.2	11.1	63	38	28
Wages and salaries	6.1	6.3	0.1	6.2	59	41	33
Other	6.0	6.0	—	4.9	57	43	28
Interest	4.0	3.9	−0.1	3.6	39	61	35
Subsidies and transfers	3.2	3.2	−0.1	3.2	61	39	29
Other	5.1	5.4	0.2	3.6	62	38	21
Capital expenditure and net lending	9.3	8.7	−0.6	8.1	31	69	36
	← In percent of total expenditure and net lending[4] →						
Total expenditure and net lending							
Current expenditure	65.4	66.9	1.5	67.8	67	33	36
Goods and services	40.5	42.0	1.5	40.9	71	29	28
Wages and salaries	22.4	23.1	0.7	23.5	66	34	33
Other	19.5	20.2	0.7	18.0	74	26	29
Interest	13.5	13.2	−0.2	13.5	42	58	35
Subsidies and transfers	9.6	10.3	0.4	11.4	65	35	31
Other	17.9	19.3	1.4	15.3	70	30	20
Capital expenditure and net lending	34.0	32.0	−1.9	31.5	28	72	36

Sources: Country authorities; and IMF staff estimates.

[1]Figures may not equal the difference between the first two columns, since they represent an average of outcomes from program targets for each sample country.

[2]Latest year for most countries is 1994–95.

[3]Number of countries for which data are available for a given expenditure category. If the sample size varies for different columns, maximum figure is given.

[4]The sum of the expenditure component may be different from 100 because of differences in sample size.

mobilize these funds.[36] This may indicate that initial targets, especially for current expenditures, were much more ambitious than those set on an annual basis, and that underperformance vis-à-vis initial three-year targets was much larger than indicated by deviations from the annual targets.[37]

---

[36]In the Kyrgyz Republic, a much sharper-than-expected economic contraction made initial program targets for expenditure, expressed as a percentage of GDP, virtually meaningless. In Ghana, original program targets for capital spending had to be revised downward because of adverse developments on the revenue side, but actual capital spending was well below this lower revised figure. In Bolivia, original program targets for capital spending were revised upward to reflect new information regarding project implementation capacity and the ability to mobilize foreign financing, but actual spending exceeded even the revised targets. In Zimbabwe, on the other hand, actual spending was closer to original targets, as projected savings in the annual program (from lower-than-expected drought-related spending) were not realized.

[37]Some caution must be used in making these comparisons, given the difference in sample size and country coverage.

Expenditure Composition

Countries with SAF/ESAF-supported programs significantly changed the composition of spending in the direction programmed. This may partly reflect the attention paid to issues of budgeting and expenditure management under SAF/ESAF programs. There was some shift in expenditure from current to capital, but not to the extent projected. Programs anticipated that capital spending and net lending would increase from 28.9 percent of total spending in the preprogram period to 34 percent during the program. In the event, capital spending rose to 32 percent of total spending. The average underspending by SAF/ESAF countries relative to program objectives reflected shortfalls in capital expenditure of 0.6 percent of GDP, with current spending as programmed.[38] Capital spending

---

[38]Capital spending fell short of program in 64 percent of the cases, and current spending in 42 percent of the cases.

Figure 8. Expenditure Performance Relative to Program Targets
(As percent of GDP)

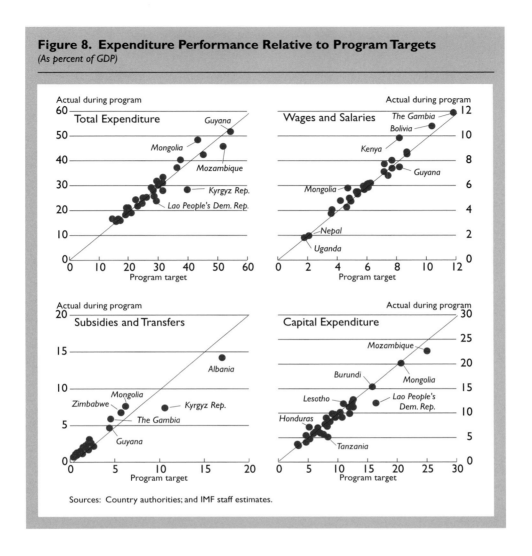

Sources: Country authorities; and IMF staff estimates.

was affected by revenue shortfalls, less-than-expected flows of foreign financing, or overly optimistic assessments of project implementation capacity (e.g., Lao People's Democratic Republic, Mozambique, and Tanzania). This was particularly true in Africa, where current expenditure exceeded program targets, while capital spending fell well short of expectations, on average; in other SAF/ESAF countries, shortfalls in total spending reflected both lower capital and current spending. For transition countries, shortfalls in capital spending were more pronounced than the SAF/ESAF countries as a whole.

Notwithstanding underperformance vis-à-vis average program targets, half of the countries in the sample were able to increase capital spending as a share of GDP. In fact, capital spending was higher, on average, during programs than in the preprogram period. In some countries, overruns in capital spend-

ing were exacerbated by poor control and monitoring of expenditure, or the failure of the budget to fully capture all expenditure (Zimbabwe and Bolivia, and Ghana in its second ESAF). Since the inception of programs, SAF/ESAF countries have managed to increase their levels of capital spending in relation to GDP. In addition, program implementation of the capital budget appears to have improved. It is impossible to know whether the productivity of public investment was maintained or increased for the SAF/ESAF countries, on average. The ability to improve the quality of public investment depends largely on improvements in budget and expenditure management practices and institutions. As noted below, there has been improvement in this area, although perhaps not fully to the extent expected.

Within current spending, wages and salaries in relation to GDP were, on average, slightly higher than targeted (e.g., in Bolivia, Kenya, and Mongolia) but substantially lower than the three-year preprogram average. About one-third of the decline in current spending as a share of total spending for SAF/ESAF countries is due to a reduction in the share of wages and salaries, and the wage bill declined as a share of total spending. This largely reflects the experience of CFA franc zone countries, which reduced wages and salaries by 2.0 percentage points of GDP, approximately as programmed.

The experience with civil service reform was mixed (Box 7). Many countries were able to achieve reductions in employment, although in some countries it grew substantially (Table 7). For 22 countries for which data are available, the average decrease in employment each year was about ½ of 1 percent, with 14 countries decreasing employment. In light of population growth, this implies a decline in government employment per capita. In many instances, however, reductions in the wage bill tended to rely more on cutbacks in real wages, and less on employment reductions, than planned; this reflected, among other things, a reluctance to carry out reforms in the face of limited job opportunities in the private sector. For 18 countries for which data are available, the average annual decrease in real wages was about 1 percent, suggesting that real wage cuts played a critical role in reducing the wage bill.[39]

ESAF countries trimmed public sector employment through different means, including limits on new recruitment (Mali), early retirement or more strictly enforced retirement rules (Ghana and Senegal), voluntary departure programs (Ghana, Lao People's Democratic Republic, and Zimbabwe), and retrenchment (Ghana and The Gambia). There were some successes as well in rationalizing administrative structures, allowing substantial employment reductions (Benin and Uganda). In addition, countries succeeded in eliminating or reducing the number of "ghost workers" and unfilled positions (11,000 ghost workers in Ghana and 40,000 in Uganda), although ghost workers remained a problem elsewhere (Burkina Faso until 1995). Retrenchment programs, however, were often less successful or more costly than envisaged. Compensation packages tended to be overly generous and poorly designed, with severance payments often increasing too rapidly with years of employment, which encouraged the most senior and skilled civil servants to leave the public sector, increasing the fiscal cost of the reform

(Uganda and Sri Lanka). In some cases, reductions in government employment were offset, in part or in full, by new hires (Bolivia, Kenya, Ghana, and Sri Lanka). In at least one instance, the target for the reduction in civil service employment was met through reduction in positions, rather than employees (Zimbabwe). Efforts to generate financial savings through retrenchment were sometimes negated by countries hiring at the higher end of the wage scale while reducing lower-level positions.[40]

A number of countries have achieved some success in correcting distortions in the civil wage structure and wage policy, although results vary widely and in some cases distortions have worsened. While some countries were able to increase the ratio between the highest and lowest paid civil servant (Ghana and Uganda), others saw this differential fall (Guinea and Senegal). Similarly, efforts to cut nonwage benefits were limited. Some countries took steps to eliminate such benefits (Guinea), but others increased the share of nonwage benefits in compensation (The Gambia and Senegal), and there is no evidence of an overall decline in these benefits. In other countries, overruns in the wage bill have been an issue, owing to inadequate budget monitoring (Togo), the granting of real wage increases because of political pressures (Bolivia), or excessive promotions (Guyana). Furthermore, the decline in real wages in many countries may have further impeded the ability of the public sector to attract qualified staff for skilled positions.[41]

Overall, a much greater emphasis was placed on securing fiscal savings than on establishing or strengthening institutions (in particular, those given responsibility to implement civil service reform) to support or sustain employment and wage reductions and to improve the efficiency and effectiveness of the government. Among the principal weaknesses of these institutions were a lack of trained personnel, inadequate or unclear authority to carry out reform, and weak expenditure control systems in the public sector, in particular payroll systems. The elements contributing to success include a strong institution to monitor and implement reform continuously (the Office of the Head of the Civil Service in Ghana), an improved payroll control system early on (Uganda), and periodic functional reviews of government (Ghana and Uganda).

Expenditures for subsidies and transfers in relation to GDP were as targeted. Spending on subsidies and transfers by SAF/ESAF countries declined as a

---

[39]This average figure excludes Uganda, where real wage growth was over 17 percent a year. Data for 13 African countries (ESAF and others) show a decline of 20 percent in central government average wages relative to per capita GDP between the early 1980s and early 1990s (see Schiavo-Campo and others, 1997a, 1997b).

[40]For more details on civil service reform, see Dia (1993) and Nunberg and Nellis (1995).

[41]A more detailed analysis of real wage developments relative to the private sector would be needed to assess fully the loss of competitiveness of the public sector.

Box 7. Challenge of Civil Service Reform

In virtually all SAF/ESAF countries, civil service reform constituted an important element of program design. Progress has been mixed, however, with employment often falling by less than programmed, reflecting the lack of perseverance with reforms in the face of scarce employment opportunities in the private sector.

Bolivia: Higher-than-programmed wages were attributable to real wage increments above those incorporated in programs, often in response to politically powerful groups, such as the armed forces and workers in the education and health sectors. The level of public sector employment appears to have played a limited role in the increase in the wage bill. In spite of severance payments of about 0.3 percent of GDP a year in 1994 and 1995, general government employment was not appreciably reduced.

Ghana: Partial progress was made on civil service reform during the country's first ESAF program. The differential between highest- and lowest-paid civil servants widened from 5.4:1 to 9.4:1 between 1988 and 1990. However, budgeted increases in real wages were eroded by higher-than-expected inflation. Some 50,000 mainly low-skilled public employees were laid off during 1987–90, with a net reduction of 30,000, or 10 percent of the civil service. This was in line with the original program's intentions. Over time, however, the reduction in public employment was largely offset by increased employment, particularly in the education sector, and this issue is being revisited in the second ESAF program.[1] New hirings (of unknown size) were also made at the local levels in 1993–95 as called for under the new constitution. The government wage bill was maintained as programmed under the second ESAF program, despite intense political pressure for wage increases and an extended strike by university teachers. The government has commissioned a study to once again develop a public sector wage policy to limit total wage payments and attract highly skilled workers. In addition, a program is being developed for reducing the civil service

by consolidating functions, eliminating duplication, and privatizing certain activities.

Kyrgyz Republic: Wages and salaries increased sharply over 1993–95, to 7.1 percent from 4.9 percent of GDP, and to 26 percent from 13 percent of total spending, despite efforts to limit nominal wage increases. The government was largely unsuccessful in its initial attempts at civil service reform.[2] While real wages at each level of the civil service declined, there was an upward shift in the structure of wage payments due to automatic promotions and reassignments. Wages as a percentage of GDP remained within the program target, although this was accompanied by the accumulation of substantial wage arrears (1.5 percent of GDP). Wage drift accounted for some 20 percent of the entire public sector wage bill increase in 1994.

Zimbabwe: Most expenditure targets for the wage bill were met under the ESAF, but all targets for reducing the size of the civil service were missed. Instead, real wages initially declined. While wages for staff in low grades were still quite high, ultimately wage compression became a problem. The number of civil service posts reached the intended level of 171,000 in spring 1996, down from 191,000 in 1991/92, with retrenchment limited to the nonsocial sectors. However, since retrenchment targeted the number of civil service posts rather than actual staff, the first-year target largely involved the elimination of vacant posts, and the decline in the total number of posts overstated the overall achievement in this area.[3] In addition, retrenchment was not based on a well-thought-out plan.[4] Severance packages were overly generous and often resulted in the loss of the most able staff in priority areas such as tax administration.

---

[2]Although the government started implementing some reductions (14 percent) of managerial positions at both republican and local levels, these positions accounted for less than 7.5 percent of the civil service.

[3]Civil service workers were reduced to 174,000 in 1995/96 from 175,000 in 1991/92 .

[4]The World Bank did not assist in the design of the retrenchment plan.

---

[1]As part of the civil service reform, the Ghanaian authorities shifted tertiary education institutions outside the civil service. University teachers' salaries are no longer linked to civil service salaries.

---

share of all spending by almost 3 percentage points, and by greater amounts for the transition economies. ESAF countries in Africa had less success in reducing subsidies (e.g., The Gambia and Zimbabwe); although such spending did decline, it did so by less than programmed. The reform of consumer subsidies and transfers has played an important role in a number of countries. Improved targeting of generalized consumer subsidies (Kyrgyz Republic), and a reduction in budgetary transfers to enterprises (the jute sector in Bangladesh), contributed to a lowering of such spending. In some cases, however, targeting

proved difficult to implement or did not generate the expected savings (Sri Lanka).

Spending on other goods and services was unchanged, as programmed, at 6 percent of GDP. The extent to which spending on operations and maintenance was protected, as planned in a number of programs, cannot be known because data are not available at this level of disaggregation. Although interest outlays were within the program targets, their share in total spending rose by around 1 percentage point.

While programs typically do not include spending targets for functional categories of expenditure,

Table 7. Changes in Government Employment and Real Wages

	Period[1]	Preprogram Employment	Latest Year Employment[2]	Employment Percentage change	Employment Annualized change	Real Wage Percentage change	Real Wage Annualized change	Coverage[3]
Albania	1992–94	212,700	169,200	−20.45	−10.81	...	...	C
Benin	1988–95	46,280	32,277	−30.26	−5.02	10.31	1.41	C
Bolivia[4]	1986–95	191,866	181,498	−5.40	−0.62	103.98	8.24	G
Burkina Faso	1990–95	33,518	39,752	18.60	3.47	−32.76	−7.63	C
Burundi	1991–95	29,500	29,138	−1.23	−0.31	−14.35	−3.80	C
Cambodia[5]	1994–95	150,000	143,855	−4.10	−4.10	...	...	G
Côte d'Ivoire	1993–95	108,300	103,200	−4.71	−2.38	−19.59	−10.33	C
Gambia, The	1985/86–1994/95	10,834	10,489	−3.19	−0.36	6.85	0.74	C
Ghana[6]	1986–95	331,579	330,000	−0.48	−0.05	62.07	5.51	C
Guinea	1991–95	50,000	52,504	5.01	1.23	4.33	1.06	C
Kenya	1986/87–1994/95	431,540	483,000	11.92	1.42	−20.99	−2.90	C
Lesotho	1989/90–1994/95	22,380	29,963	33.88	6.01	3.65	0.72	C
Madagascar	1986–95	129,500	114,189	−11.82	−1.39	−14.37	−1.71	C
Mali[7]	1987–94	52,787	32,719	−38.02	−6.60	39.26	4.85	C
Mauritania	1985–94	18,209	20,344	11.72	1.24	−45.19	−6.46	C
Niger	1988/89–1994	35,000	40,000	14.29	2.46	−5.56	−1.04	C
Senegal	1985/86–1995	68,843	67,049	−2.61	−0.28	6.42	0.66	C
Sri Lanka	1988–95	464,000	738,000	59.05	6.85	−0.82	−0.12	C
Togo[8]	1987–94	32,256	32,032	−0.69	−0.10	−14.40	−2.20	C
Uganda	1984/85–1994/95	266,000	150,000	−43.61	−5.57	405.80	17.60	C
Vietnam	1993–95	1,207,000	1,258,000	4.23	2.09	...	...	G
Zimbabwe[9]	1991/92–1994/95	241,511	236,860	−1.93	−0.65	−9.51	−3.28	C
Average[10]				−0.44	−0.61	3.29	−0.90	
Africa				−2.54	−0.40	−2.74	−1.52	
CFA franc countries				−6.20	−1.21	−2.33	−2.04	
Other				−0.03	0.16	−3.06	−1.12	
Median[10]				−1.58	−0.29	−3.19	−0.58	
Africa				−1.23	−0.28	−7.54	−1.37	
CFA franc countries				−2.61	−0.28	−5.56	−1.04	
Other				−0.85	−0.18	−9.51	−1.71	

Sources: Country authorities; and IMF staff estimates. In cases in which fiscal years were different from calendar years, employment figures were adjusted to be consistent with the fiscal year.

[1]Earliest year corresponds to preprogram year, or, if data are not available, to year closest to the preprogram year.

[2]Latest year for which data are available.

[3](C) indicates central government; (G), general.

[4]Preprogram employment figures have been adjusted to ensure the same coverage as 1995 data.

[5]Excludes the military.

[6]Staff estimates for 1995.

[7]Figures for employment include temporary workers and employment by regional governments. Figures on real wages should be interpreted with caution, as the wages of regional government workers are excluded from the wage bill.

[8]Real wage figures should be interpreted with caution, as the military is excluded from employment but included in the wage bill calculations.

[9]Staff estimates of employment in the military and police are used to estimate total central government employment.

[10]Comprises 22 countries for employment and 18 for wages. Uganda is excluded from the average real wage calculations.

changes in such spending categories suggest that expenditure allocation may have improved over the program period. Comparing the most recent year for which data are available with the three-year preprogram average, we found that SAF/ESAF countries re-

duced military spending and expenditures on general public services such as planning and printing (Table 8 and Appendix Table 28) and outside of Africa on economic services such as energy, mining, and manufacturing (Appendix Table 29), while increasing social

Table 8. Summary of Expenditure by Function
(Averages of SAF/ESAF country samples)

	Average of Three Years Prior to Program	Pre-program Year	Latest Year (1994 or 1995)	Latest Year Minus Three-Year Pre-program Average[1]	Latest Year Minus Pre-program Year[1]	Number of Countries[2]
	In percent of GDP[3]					
Total expenditure and net lending	29.0	27.6	26.1	−2.6	−1.6	36
General public services	3.5	3.5	3.2	−0.4	−0.3	19
Military spending	2.9	2.9	2.5	−0.4	−0.4	26
Education	3.6	3.6	4.2	0.3	0.5	23
Health	1.6	1.6	2.0	0.3	0.4	23
Social security and welfare	1.9	1.9	1.8	—	0.3	17
Housing	0.8	0.5	0.6	−0.2	0.1	11
Economic services	5.0	5.1	4.9	−0.2	0.3	19
Transportation and communication	1.5	1.2	1.3	−0.1	0.2	13
	In percent of total expenditure and net lending					
Total expenditure and net lending						
General public services	14.9	14.7	13.9	−2.6	−2.4	19
Military spending	13.0	12.0	11.3	−1.7	−1.4	26
Education	13.8	14.3	16.0	1.5	1.8	23
Health	5.8	6.1	7.4	1.1	1.3	23
Social security and welfare	6.4	6.7	6.1	—	0.8	17
Housing	3.0	2.1	2.5	−0.3	0.4	11
Economic services	19.6	19.8	18.7	−1.2	0.2	19
Transportation and communication	6.2	4.6	5.5	−0.2	1.2	13

Sources: IMF, *Government Finance Statistics Yearbook* (1995) and staff estimates; and country authorities.

[1]Figures may not equal the difference between the latest year and the preprogram values because they represent an average of deviation of outcomes from preprogram values for each sample country.

[2]Number of countries for which data are available for a given expenditure category. If the sample size varies for different columns, the maximum figure is given.

[3]The sum of expenditure components may differ from totals because of differences in sample size and the fact that net lending and other items may be excluded from the functional categories.

spending (see below, "Social Aspects of Expenditure Policy").[42] The decline in spending on economic services likely reflects, in part, the decreasing role of government in productive sectors of the economy, while lower spending on general services may reflect declining administrative costs.

Military spending declined for SAF/ESAF countries, falling from 2.9 percent of GDP in the three-year preprogram average to 2.5 percent for the latest year for which data are available, and declining for three-fourths of the countries (Appendix Table 30). This decline mirrored a worldwide trend toward lower military spending.[43] Cuts in military spending were larger for SAF/ESAF countries in Africa, at 0.6 percent of GDP. Reductions in military spending were incorporated in some ESAF-supported pro-

grams, stemming from improvements in regional security (Zimbabwe) or internal security (Togo), and a demobilization of soldiers that freed resources for high-priority social spending (Uganda).

SAF/ESAF countries may have reduced recorded total spending below programmed levels by modifying some other aspect of fiscal behavior for which comprehensive data are not available. For instance, governments may have pushed some spending off-budget (e.g., public enterprise losses in Zimbabwe), increased implicit subsidies or quasi-fiscal operations of public financial institutions to offset declines in subsidies and transfers, or increased arrears or contingent liabilities, perhaps, through the provision of government guarantees. Similarly, some new spending obligations taken over in the context of bank restructuring may not be fully accounted for, or their treatment in fiscal accounts may have changed during the program period. It may also be the case— although, again, data are not widely available—that changes in spending at the national level may have

---

[42]The decline in spending on general public and economic services is traceable to CFA franc zone countries.

[43]See Gupta, Schiff, and Clements (1996).

affected local government spending, for example, as intergovernmental transfers declined or the provision of certain public services was shifted to local levels. This may suggest that the shifts between capital and current outlays indicated by budgetary data are distorted.

Mid-Course Corrections

SAF/ESAF countries typically took two types of mid-course corrective actions. First, they responded to revenue shortfalls by cutting expenditures across the board, so as to meet fiscal targets. A number of countries adopted the system of cash rationing in response to revenue shortfalls, which, in turn, led to the accumulation of expenditure arrears of as much as 5 percent of GDP. It also engendered inefficiencies in expenditure allocations by continuing to support low-priority programs while depriving high-priority ones, such as for operations and maintenance of budgetary allocations (Kyrgyz Republic). In other cases, expenditure cuts focused on capital spending (Ghana). Second, countries responded by offsetting expenditure overruns in one area with cutbacks in others. For instance, overruns in wage payments were compensated for by cuts in other current spending (Bolivia). In other cases, countries did not respond and fiscal targets were missed, contributing to a failure to complete a program review (Bolivia, in 1993). Elsewhere, expenditure measures were agreed to but not implemented, contributing to the failure to complete programs (Zimbabwe).

Expenditure Management

Problems of poor budgeting, lax expenditure control and evaluation, inadequate institutions, too few trained personnel, and weak political commitment have consistently led to the failure to implement envisaged structural reforms, such as civil service reforms and reform of public investment programs (Box 8). These problems have also contributed to difficulties in meeting expenditure targets, either in terms of levels or composition. The prevalence of extrabudgetary funds, the separation between capital and current budgets, and the inability of the ministry of finance to control wages have led to spending overruns and inefficiencies (Togo). The lack of budget monitoring and evaluation has limited governments' ability to improve expenditure productivity, resulting in spending overruns and the buildup of arrears in the capital budget (Ghana and Kenya). Weak or nonexistent expenditure control mechanisms, including at the subnational levels, and parliamentary approval of unbudgeted expenditures have caused fiscal targets to be missed or large ex-

penditure arrears to accumulate (Kyrgyz Republic, Malawi, and Zimbabwe).

The IMF has frequently provided technical assistance to strengthen expenditure management, in many cases in conjunction with the World Bank. In a number of countries (such as the Kyrgyz Republic) programs included the establishment of a treasury to enhance the overall control of expenditure. In other cases, specific measures were included as benchmarks, such as adopting a World Bank-approved public investment program (Togo), or requiring that the budget be integrated with the fiscal program (Bolivia). However, problems have proved more intractable than envisaged in many programs. In fact, even when benchmarks were met and the requisite institutions set up, problems in policy formulation often persisted (Kyrgyz Republic). This may, in part, reflect a lack of both political will and administrative capacity.[44] Nevertheless, sustained technical assistance from the IMF and the Bank in recent years has significantly improved the ability of ESAF countries to undertake structural reforms.

Sequencing of Expenditure Policies

The sequencing of expenditure policy often differed from that envisaged in programs. Many programs attempted to reform expenditure policy and strengthen public expenditure management simultaneously. However, delays in implementing fundamental changes in one or both areas often resulted in the generation of expenditure arrears (Kyrgyz Republic) or outlays that were not fully reflected in recorded expenditure (Zimbabwe), and made meeting budgetary targets more difficult (e.g., wages in Togo). In some cases, problems in public expenditure management emerged after program targets were missed (Bolivia and Zimbabwe), generating requests for IMF technical assistance. In other cases, stabilization was viewed as occurring before structural reforms, but the needed expenditure cuts were—in the absence of such reforms—either not forthcoming or undertaken in an inefficient manner. For instance, targets to reduce the wage bill, in the absence of a well-thought-out plan for civil service reform, led to lower real wages and increased wage compression.

Sustainability of Expenditure Reforms

To what extent were the expenditure reforms made under ESAF-supported programs sustained? This question is difficult to answer unequivocally since a large number of ESAF programs are still ongoing.

---

[44]For instance, lack of skilled staff has been identified as a constraint to reform in Lesotho.

Box 8. Improving Public Expenditure Management

Progress has been made in strengthening public expenditure management in a number of countries, but shortcomings have persisted, contributing to difficulties in meeting expenditure targets.

Ghana: The first ESAF program stressed strengthening expenditure management. Since 1986, progress has been made in rationalizing budget procedures, with assistance from the World Bank and the IMF. However, expenditure management is still a problem, as indicated by capital spending overruns. The benchmarks included in the second ESAF program, for the development of a new budget and expenditure tracking and monitoring system, and its implementation in the six largest ministries, were met. New procedures are designed to improve monitoring of expenditure commitments (including by the ministry of roads and highways), extend quarterly budget reviews to all spending agencies, and introduce new contracting and procurement procedures to enhance transparency and increase value for money.

Kyrgyz Republic: The development of the treasury, supported by IMF technical assistance, has significantly enhanced government control over public expenditure and cash management. The treasury, now fully in operation, has achieved comprehensive coverage of government finance including the budgetary as well as extrabudgetary activities of both republican and local governments. In addition, a new government payment system has been introduced, and a treasury single account established at the central bank, replacing over 5,000 separate bank accounts. Monthly and annual reports on all fiscal operations passing through the treasury are now generated.

Togo: The lack of transparency in the financial operations of the government has led to overspending, distortions in expenditure composition, and arrears, which reached 9 percent of GDP in 1987. About 40 percent of all government financial operations are effected through "suspense accounts," which are regularized only occasionally. Moreover, ministries have accounts in private

banks, which are beyond the control of the ministry of finance, rendering the treasury consolidation arduous and cash management impossible.[1] Moreover, budget execution is unduly complicated, leading spending ministries to bypass the ministry of finance's normal approval procedures frequently and encouraging arrears. Finally, financial deadlines are frequently not met. For instance, the 1994 budget was passed in September 1994, and the 1995 budget was passed in February but implemented only in June. The advance accounts used to finance expenditure until the budget can be executed are seldom regularized. Despite these problems, the ESAF-supported programs appear to have been moderately successful in tackling domestic and external arrears, which have been reduced from high preprogram levels but nevertheless remain large. Programs were not entirely successful in streamlining budgetary procedures relating to special accounts, and thus, the formulation of fiscal policy remains problematic.

Zimbabwe: The lack of proper expenditure control mechanisms and regular parliamentary approval for expenditure overruns undermined spending discipline and resulted in frequent overruns on nonwage goods and services and transfer payments. Budgets were not prepared within a medium-term framework, and frequent ex post revisions softened the budget constraint. The introduction of quarterly expenditure ceilings in fiscal year 1994/95 proved ineffective. Weak budgetary institutions also facilitated the shift of major expenditure items off budget. Only in October 1995, after the expiration of the ESAF, did the authorities introduce an effective cash-management facility as a first step to a broader computerized commitment control system.

---

[1]In early 1995, some accounts were closed and the treasury began to follow up on these operations, which slightly improved the flow of financial information.

However, a comparison of average spending during programs (averaging five years) with spending in the latest year for all program countries for which data are available indicates that while broad changes in spending levels and composition made during the programs were largely maintained, some slippages did occur. For instance, where total spending declined as a share of GDP during the typical ESAF and fell short of programmed levels, such spending continued to fall over the course of, and after, the program—by an additional 1.6 percent of GDP, on average. Capital spending, which fell significantly short of program targets, continued to fall, by an additional 0.6 percent of GDP. In Africa, where capital spending declines were particularly severe, the dropoff was also larger, at 0.9 percent of GDP. Spending on other goods and ser-

vices, which was in line with expectations for the program years, declined by 0.9 percent of GDP in the most recent year. To the extent that this included cuts in spending on operations and maintenance, it may have adversely affected the capital stock. In Ghana, for instance, many of the gains from civil service reform during the first ESAF-supported program dissipated, as employment levels increased and wages rose sharply as a share of GDP. Many of the issues that seemingly were addressed during the first SAF/ESAF are now under study again.

Completed versus Interrupted Programs

The issue of sustainability is also addressed by asking how expenditure policy differed between countries where three successful reviews were completed and those where programs were not completed.[45] This is relevant because excess public spending is more likely to be associated with breaching of performance criteria for net domestic financing of the public sector than expenditure shortfalls are, other things being equal. For the 12 countries failing to complete their programs, total spending was slightly higher than programmed, because overruns in current spending more than offset large shortfalls in capital spending of 1 percent of GDP. Wages and salaries exceeded program targets, by 0.3 percent of GDP, and interest payments were larger than expected, by 0.2 percent of GDP, though the outcome for subsidies and transfers was similar to that in completed programs. In addition, other current spending averaged some 0.6 percent of GDP more than programmed, perhaps reflecting unforeseen spending needs in a number of countries. For the 14 countries that successfully completed SAF/ESAF programs, on the other hand, total expenditure during the programs was lower than programmed, by 0.6 percent of GDP, with 0.5 percent of GDP of the shortfall in capital spending. Within current spending, wages and salaries were in line with what was programmed, while subsidies and transfers exceeded program levels by 0.2 percent of GDP, and interest was below program by the same amount.

The number of program interruptions is also significant for sustainability. Countries that had no interruptions in SAF/ESAF-supported programs (including some programs that have not yet been completed) have tended to underspend relative to program targets by more than SAF/ESAF countries as a whole, with total spending falling short of program by an average of 1.7 percentage points of GDP (Table 9). In addition, these countries have made large shifts in expenditure composition, from current to capital, compared both with other SAF/ESAF countries and with programmed expenditure shifts. In fact, these countries were able to increase capital spending to programmed levels while reducing current spending substantially more than programmed. The lower-than-programmed current spending is in part due to reduced interest payments—which may in turn reflect lower borrowing costs or write-offs on interest payments—but also to lower spending on other goods and services and other current spending.

We found that overruns on current spending, at least partly stemming from failure to make structural reforms, hindered the completion of programs. For example, for countries with three or more program interruptions, current spending was higher than programmed by 0.8 percent of GDP, with spending overruns in all categories of current spending, and capital spending was lower than programmed by the same amount. At the same time, revenue was lower by 0.6 percent of GDP and total spending was higher than programmed by 0.3 percent of GDP.

Social Aspects of Expenditure Policy

This section addresses the extent to which SAF/ESAF countries were able to maintain or increase social spending and examines developments in social indicators and implementation of social safety nets. The data suggest that, on average, spending on education and health in SAF/ESAF countries fared reasonably well during program periods, although substantially less so in CFA franc zone countries. Social indicators have also improved, although performance varied considerably from country to country. These results should be interpreted with caution because, in some cases, spending increases represent small absolute changes in relation to low initial levels, although average social spending in relation to GDP during preprogram periods was not markedly different from that prevailing in middle-income countries. Note that data on social spending are available for only about two-thirds of the SAF/ESAF countries in the sample, and social indicator data are often available for relatively small samples.

Changes in Social Spending

Education spending increased in real terms by an average of 46 percent, comparing the most recent year for which data are available with the preprogram year, a period that averaged six years (Appendix Table 31). This implies an average annual growth rate of 6.4 percent a year, and an average annual per capita growth rate of 3.8 percent (Appendix Table 32 and Figure 9).[46] Over 85 percent of the 23 countries in the sample for which data are available raised real spending, and almost 75 percent increased real per capita spending. Average education spending also increased as a share of GDP by 0.5 percent of GDP, rising for over 75 percent of the countries (Appendix Table 33 and Figure 10). Relatively low increases in spending in relation to GDP, in contrast with real spending increases, reflect GDP growth and low levels of initial spending in some countries. In addition, education spending rose significantly as a share of total spending (Appendix

---

[45]A third category of programs, those still in progress, are not discussed here.

[46]Excluding Cambodia and Nicaragua, which experienced very high increases in spending over a short time span, the average annual rate of growth of real education spending was 4.5 percent, and per capita annual growth was 1.9 percent.

Table 9. Expenditure: Summary of Program Implementation by Number of Program Interruptions[1]

(In percent of GDP; averages of SAF/ESAF country samples)

	Number of Program Interruptions[2]			
	0	1	2	3
Average expenditure during program minus average program target				
Total expenditure and net lending	−1.7	0.4	−0.7	0.3
Current expenditure	−1.7	0.9	0.2	0.8
Goods and services	−0.8	0.8	—	0.8
Wages and salaries	—	0.3	0.1	0.3
Other	−0.8	0.5	—	0.4
Interest	−0.3	—	−0.1	0.1
Subsidies and transfers	−1.0	0.4	0.1	0.3
Other	−0.4	0.7	0.2	0.2
Capital expenditure and net lending	—	−0.6	−0.9	−0.8
Latest year minus preprogram average[3]				
Total expenditure and net lending	−1.4	−1.7	−2.2	−0.2
Current expenditure	−1.9	−3.9	−1.5	0.6
Goods and services	1.2	−2.5	−1.7	1.2
Wages and salaries	—	−0.4	−1.1	1.3
Other	0.4	−0.9	−0.5	−1.2
Interest	−0.2	−1.2	0.6	−0.5
Subsidies and transfers	−4.2	−0.4	−0.5	0.5
Other	−0.5	−0.3	−0.2	−1.1
Capital expenditure and net lending	0.4	1.9	−0.4	−0.9

Sources: Country authorities; and IMF staff estimates.

[1]A *program interruption* is defined as either an interval of more than six months between different IMF arrangements, an interval of more than six months between annual arrangements, or a delay of more than six months in completing an ESAF program review.

[2]The data include 8 countries with no interruptions, 10 countries with one interruption, 12 countries with two interruptions, and 6 countries with three interruptions.

[3]Latest year for which data are available.

Table 34), suggesting that education became a higher priority for SAF/ESAF countries.

These results, however, obscure the considerable variations among countries. First, spending increases were considerably smaller among SAF/ESAF countries in Africa than for other SAF/ESAF countries, despite the rapid population growth in this region. Real education spending rose by just 2.4 percent a year in Africa, compared with more than 11 percent a year for other SAF/ESAF countries; all three countries in the sample that reduced real education spending were in Africa (Côte d'Ivoire, Madagascar, and Mali). Real per capita spending in Africa actually declined by 0.4 percent a year, in contrast to a rise of more than 9 percent a year elsewhere; this occurred despite the fact that real per capita spending increased by considerable amounts in Burkina Faso, Ghana, and Lesotho. However, education spending did increase by 0.4 percentage points of GDP in Africa. Other SAF/ESAF countries, on the other hand, were able to increase education spending by an average of 0.8 percent of GDP, while sharply reducing total spending by 2.7 percent of GDP. The smaller increase in spending in Africa is strongly influenced by large declines in real education spending in some countries (over 17 percent a year in Côte d'Ivoire), reflecting cuts in teacher salaries from a high level.[47]

Expenditure on health care increased as well, with an average rise of nearly 56 percent in real terms, with only three countries (Côte d'Ivoire, Mali, and Vietnam) reducing such spending (Appendix Table 35). This translates into an annual average increase in real health spending of 8.4 percent, and an annual

---

[47]Real spending reductions in Mali have also been influenced by real wage cuts in the aftermath of the 1994 devaluation. Note that some countries with expenditure cuts or slow growth in real education outlays (e.g., Côte d'Ivoire and Zimbabwe) started from very high levels of initial spending relative to other ESAF countries.

Figure 9. Annual Average Change in Real Per Capita Education and Health Spending Under SAF/ESAF Programs

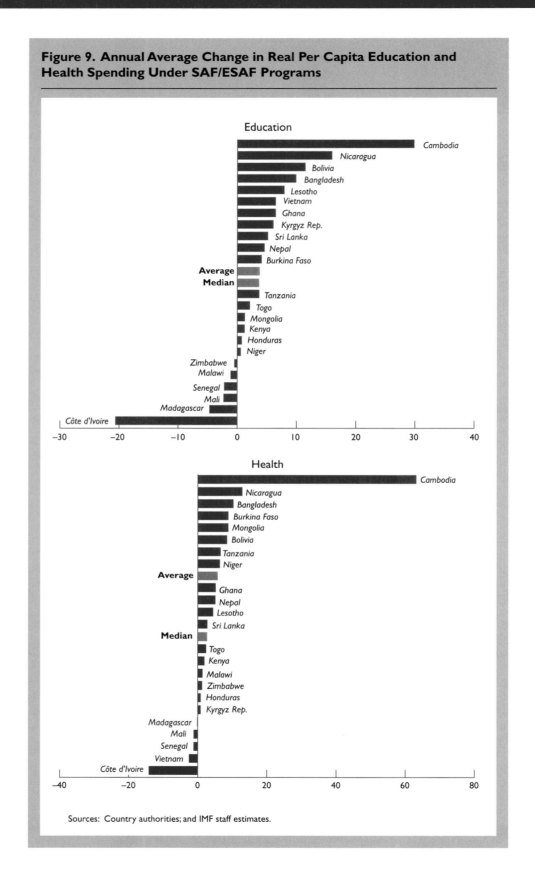

Sources: Country authorities; and IMF staff estimates.

Figure 10. Change in Education and Health Spending in Relation to GDP Under SAF/ESAF Programs[1]

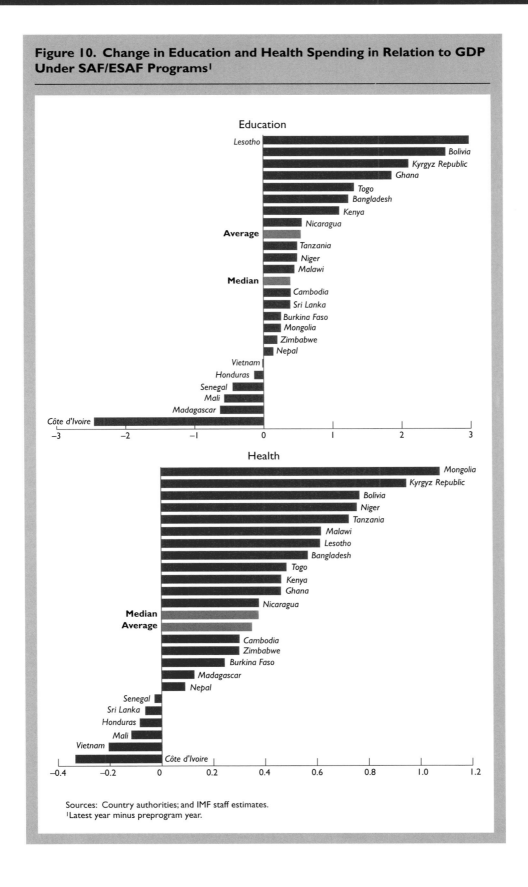

Sources: Country authorities; and IMF staff estimates.
[1]Latest year minus preprogram year.

Table 10. Social Indicators for SAF/ESAF Countries[1]
(Percent of population unless otherwise indicated)

	Average Pre-program[2]	Average Program or Postprogram[3]	Average Percent Improvement	Average Annual Percent Improvement	Median Pre-program	Median Post-program	Median Percent Improvement[4]	Number of Countries[5]		Average Years Covered[6]	Average Annual Percent Improvement in 24 Other Low-Income Countries
Education											
Illiteracy rate	56.6	51.4	13.6	3.0	(2.3)	44.0	35.4	9.4	24	(15)	6.0	4.2
Enrollment rates, in percent											
Primary school	72.0	79.1	11.6	1.1	(1.0)	107.0	93.5	3.4	26	(18)	6.6	0.6
Secondary school	21.2	22.9	12.8	1.3	(2.4)	15.0	11.0	5.6	26	(18)	6.7	2.7
Repeater rate	20.7	20.7	-21.6	-4.4	(-6.0)	27.2	27.7	1.6	12	(9)	3.7	...
Health care											
Life expectancy (years)	53.0	54.1	2.1	0.3	(0.1)	65.5	67.8	3.0	31	(20)	5.7	0.5
Infant mortality rate											
(per thousand births)	97.1	85.0	11.5	2.1	(1.5)	113.4	90.4	11.7	35	(20)	6.5	3.1
Access to health care[7]	46.2	63.7	73.7	9.7	(13.6)	13.0	45.0	64.4	7	(4)	5.6	3.4
Percent under 5 immunized:											
DPT	39.0	62.5	327.9	14.4	(15.2)	78.0	81.0	100.0	27	(19)	6.0	7.7
Measles	41.4	63.9	198.7	12.4	(5.6)	81.0	78.0	42.4	25	(15)	6.7	14.1
Other basic services											
Access to safe water[7]	40.1	50.1	39.4	5.6	(6.3)	42.0	45.0	11.7	15	(11)	5.5	2.7
Access to sanitation[7]	28.2	39.6	263.2	7.8	(5.3)	20.0	35.0	61.5	21	(14)	8.5	...
Poverty and income distribution											
Poverty rate[8]	41.9	34.0	20.5	5.3	(6.3)	43.0	32.0	23.0	7	(2)	5.4	1.1
Gini coefficient[9]	41.2	38.6	3.7	0.9	(-2.9)	42.0	37.3	-2.5	7	(2)	3.7	-0.6
Income shares[10]	7.8	7.1	7.4	2.2	(-0.6)	7.7	7.2	10.7	5	(2)	4.0	...

Sources: World Bank, Social Indicators Database and database of International Economics Department; database of Deininger and Squire (1996); Jayarajah, Branson, and Binayak (1996); and World Bank (1996b, 1996e).

[1]Figures in parentheses are for African countries.

[2]Most recent preprogram year for which data are available.

[3]Most recent year either during or after the program for which data are available.

[4]The average and median percentage improvements average individual countries' improvements, and do not equal changes between average preprogram and average program/postprogram results.

[5]Number of countries for which data are available for preprogram period and either program or postprogram period, for at least one year.

[6]Number of years between preprogram and program/postprogram data.

[7]Percent of population with local access.

[8]Data for Ghana and Honduras are for the population considered very poor, while for Bangladesh, Pakistan, Sri Lanka, and Tanzania, data refer to country-specific poverty lines. Estimates of poverty in Bolivia are based on surveys of the urban population, while for Tanzania, they rely on rural areas; estimates for other countries are for the whole country.

[9]Gini coefficients are estimated from expenditure or income data, before or after taxes, for a household or an individual. For Bangladesh and Sri Lanka, the data are from both income surveys of households and expenditure surveys of individuals, while for Pakistan, both household data and per capita data are used. Data are taken from national surveys, except for Bolivia, where only urban areas were covered.

[10]Share in total income of the richest quartile of the population divided by the income share of the poorest quartile.

rise in per capita spending of 5.8 percent (Appendix Table 36).[48] The annual median increase in real spending was 6.2 percent. Health spending rose as a share of GDP (by 0.4 percentage points) with three-fourths of the countries registering an increase (Appendix Table 37). The share of total spending accounted for by health care rose by over 1 percentage point, increasing for more than 75 percent of the countries (Appendix Table 38), implying that health care also became a higher priority under ESAF programs. Again, African countries registered smaller increases: they averaged 4.6 percent a year in real terms, compared with over 13 percent a year for other program countries, and climbed by 1.7 percent a year in real per capita terms, compared with a rise of 11 percent a year elsewhere.[49] Some African countries did, however, succeed in increasing real per capita annual spending by amounts larger than the average for all countries (Burkina Faso, Niger, and Tanzania). The median annual real increase in Africa (6.2 percent) was considerably higher than the average (4.6 percent), which was lowered by large reductions in Côte d'Ivoire.

Trends in Social Indicators

A crucial issue is whether these increases in spending have had an impact on the well-being of the population in general and of the most needy members of society in particular. A number of factors besides government spending policy affect social indicators, including general economic conditions, improvements in health technology (as reflected in long-term improvements worldwide), and the activities of nongovernmental organizations and other private sector service providers. In addition, the efficiency with which social services are provided by the government, and how precisely the truly needy are targeted, play important roles. Nevertheless, the increase in the share of spending allocated to health and education in SAF/ESAF countries coincided with tangible improvements in social indicators.[50]

Output indicators in education, for example, provide evidence of a 14 percent drop in illiteracy since the beginning of the program period, or some 3.0 percent a year, although illiteracy rates remained high by inter-

national standards (Table 10). Annual gains in literacy were somewhat smaller in Africa. Gross enrollment rates for primary and secondary education improved 1.1 percent and 1.3 percent a year, in part traceable to higher education spending in relation to GDP (Figures 10 through 12).[51] Some countries experienced relatively large annual increments in primary education enrollment, including some African countries (e.g., Burundi, Malawi, Mauritania). However, the repeater rate—a proxy for the quality of education—actually worsened, on average (although an increase in the repeater rate may also represent the application of stricter education standards). Improvements in some output indicators tended to be larger for a group of low-income countries without SAF/ESAF programs; for example, illiteracy declined in this group by over 4 percent a year, 1 percent more a year than for SAF/ESAF countries as a whole, although SAF/ESAF countries seem to have made relatively greater strides in increasing primary school enrollment.

With respect to indicators of progress in health, access to health care broadened substantially among SAF/ESAF countries, rising from 46 percent to 64 percent, or 10 percent a year. In addition, program countries raised their share of children immunized against DPT and measles by 14 percent and 12 percent a year, and sharply increased the percentage of the population with access to safe water and sanitation. In some cases, the gains exceeded those observed for the group of low-income countries without SAF/ESAF programs mentioned above. However, improvements in health status were less dramatic. Life expectancy increased by just 0.3 percent a year, about 60 percent as rapidly as a group of other low-income countries. Infant mortality rates fell by about 2.1 percent a year, again, reflecting increased health outlays as a share of GDP. Access to health care rose more sharply for African SAF/ESAF countries than for other program countries. However, gains in health status in Africa were smaller than for other program countries, with life expectancy rising 33 percent as fast, and infant mortality improving 70 percent as fast, figures that may reflect the adverse effect of AIDS on these indicators (e.g., in Uganda and Zimbabwe).

The median improvements in social indicators paint a somewhat different picture, with a much sharper drop in illiteracy and larger improvements in access to health care and sanitation, life expectancy, infant mortality rates, and repeater rates, but less favorable outcomes for school enrollment and access to safe water. This underscores the highly skewed distribution of outcomes and the need for caution in inter-

---

[48]Excluding Cambodia and Nicaragua, the average annual rate of growth of real health spending was 5.3 percent, and per capita annual growth was 2.7 percent.

[49]Two of the three countries reducing such spending are in Africa.

[50]These results should be interpreted with some caution, given the reduced sample size for which certain data for social indicators are available and the fact that data may not exactly correspond to the program period.

---

[51]The difficulty in achieving larger improvements in literacy and enrollment rates may reflect the difficulty of low-income families in keeping school-age children out of the workforce.

Figure 11. Average Annual Change in Enrollment and Infant Mortality Rates Under SAF/ESAF Programs[1]

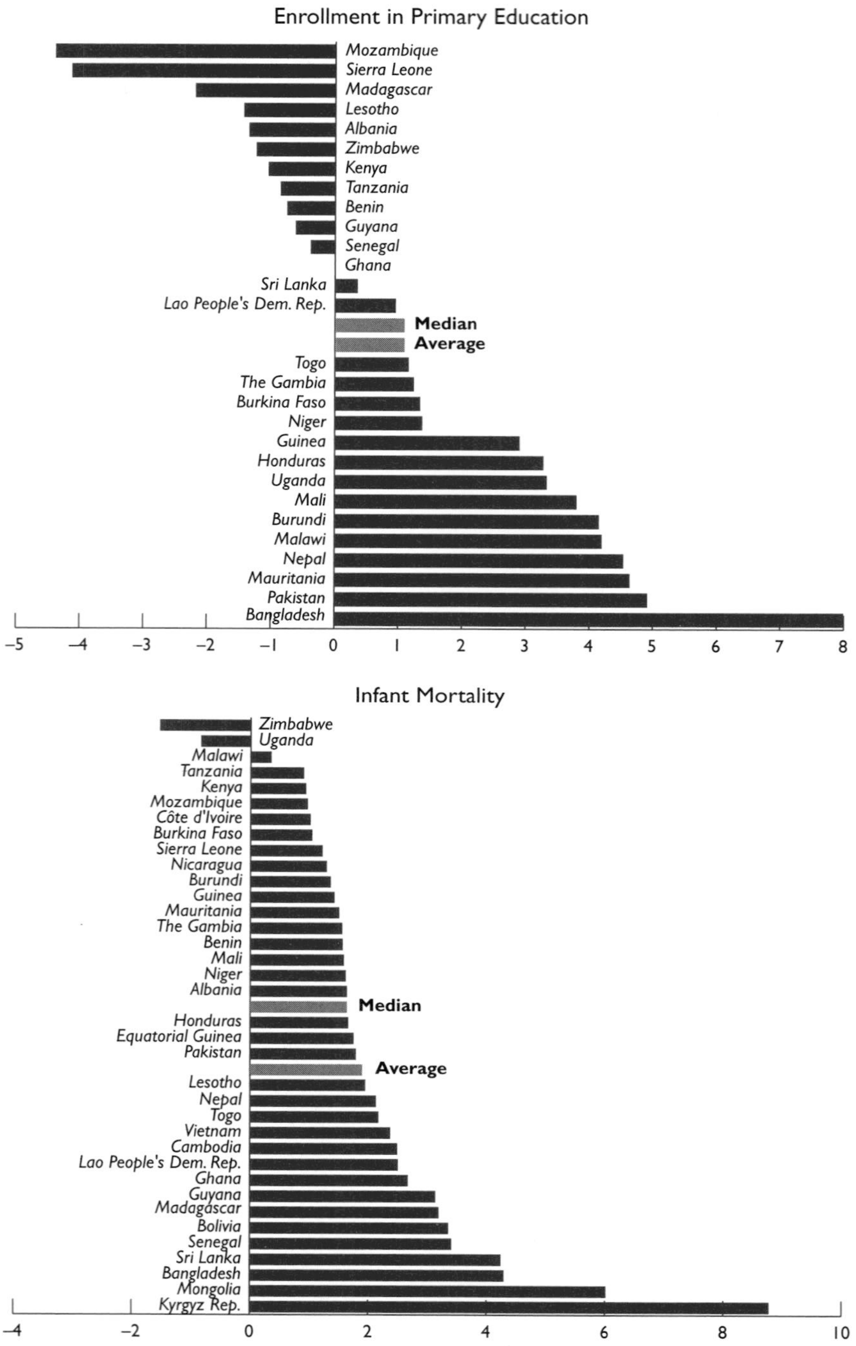

Enrollment in Primary Education

Mozambique
Sierra Leone
Madagascar
Lesotho
Albania
Zimbabwe
Kenya
Tanzania
Benin
Guyana
Senegal
Ghana
Sri Lanka
Lao People's Dem. Rep.
Median
Average
Togo
The Gambia
Burkina Faso
Niger
Guinea
Honduras
Uganda
Mali
Burundi
Malawi
Nepal
Mauritania
Pakistan
Bangladesh

−5   −4   −3   −2   −1   0   1   2   3   4   5   6   7   8

Infant Mortality

Zimbabwe
Uganda
Malawi
Tanzania
Kenya
Mozambique
Côte d'Ivoire
Burkina Faso
Sierra Leone
Nicaragua
Burundi
Guinea
Mauritania
The Gambia
Benin
Mali
Niger
Albania
Median
Honduras
Equatorial Guinea
Pakistan
Average
Lesotho
Nepal
Togo
Vietnam
Cambodia
Lao People's Dem. Rep.
Ghana
Guyana
Madagascar
Bolivia
Senegal
Sri Lanka
Bangladesh
Mongolia
Kyrgyz Rep.

−4   −2   0   2   4   6   8   10

Sources: World Bank, Social Indicators Database, and International Economics Department Database.
[1]An improvement in infant mortality rates is indicated by an increase.

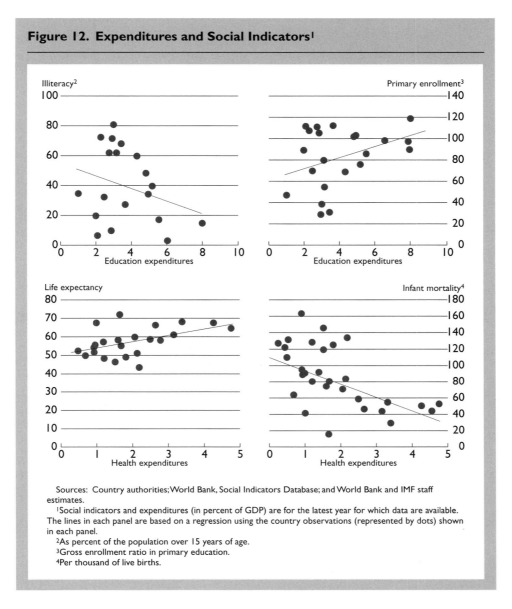

Figure 12. Expenditures and Social Indicators[1]

Sources: Country authorities; World Bank, Social Indicators Database; and World Bank and IMF staff estimates.

[1]Social indicators and expenditures (in percent of GDP) are for the latest year for which data are available. The lines in each panel are based on a regression using the country observations (represented by dots) shown in each panel.

[2]As percent of the population over 15 years of age.

[3]Gross enrollment ratio in primary education.

[4]Per thousand of live births.

preting the social indicators data, in particular where the sample size is small.

Expenditure Efficiency and Benefit Incidence

Education and health spending appear to have a positive impact on many social indicators.[52] Some countries experienced both large increases in spending and

substantial improvements in health indicators such as infant mortality rates (Bangladesh and Bolivia), while others increased spending markedly yet achieved just modest gains (Burkina Faso and Kenya).

It would appear that SAF/ESAF countries could have made further progress had more attention been paid to issues of expenditure composition and productivity (Box 9). For instance, available data on the composition of education spending for nine ESAF countries suggests that the share of education spending dedicated to primary education was virtually unchanged, at about 50 percent, during ESAF programs[53]

[52]Regressions with per capita health and education spending as independent variables are statistically significant with respect to primary and secondary enrollment rates, life expectancy, and infant mortality rates. Health and education spending lose their significance in the cases of primary enrollment and life expectancy when a variable measuring per capita income in the base year is included in the regression, in part due to a high degree of correlation between independent variables.

[53]These data, primarily from UNESCO, are not necessarily consistent with other data presented in this paper.

Box 9. Addressing Inefficiencies in Health and Education Spending

While expenditures on health and education have risen briskly in many countries since the beginning of their first SAF/ESAF program, there is considerable scope for increasing the level and efficiency of this spending and improving its benefit incidence.

Bolivia: Bolivia's high level of expenditure on education, in tandem with low education attainment levels, suggests a substantial degree of inefficiency. This inefficiency is due to both a misallocation of spending within the education sector (with substantial resources devoted to higher education) and inefficiency within each subsector. For example, from 1980 to 1995, outlays for textbooks were insignificant, and wages accounted for about 95–98 percent of primary and secondary current expenditure (compared with the Latin American average of 75 percent). Furthermore, spending on higher education increased from 0.8 percent of GDP in 1986 to about 1.5 percent of GDP in 1994. Supported by advice from the World Bank, ESAF programs have incorporated reforms of the education sector by limiting resources for postsecondary education and increasing the allocation for textbooks.[1] However, relatively little progress has been made in these areas. The targeted reduction in the share of spending allocated to higher education did not materialize. There is also evidence of some inefficiency in the health system in Bolivia, owing to the excessive allocation for curative care and the inappropriate concentration of health resources in higher-income regions. Since 1995 the ESAF program has set specific targets for primary health expenditures, but the lack of data has hampered the monitoring of progress on this front.

Ghana: In the period between the first and second ESAF programs, education spending rose dramatically. However, wages and salaries accounted for about 95 percent of current costs, leaving little for operations and maintenance and educational materials. In addition, the bottom 20 percent of the population received 16 percent of education spending in 1992, slightly lower than in 1988. Only spending on primary education was progressive, with 22 percent of spending benefiting the poorest 20 percent. Between 1987 and 1990, the share of primary education in the ministry of education's budget increased somewhat, from 40 percent to 43 percent. However, health care spending is regressive in its benefit incidence, with only an estimated 11 percent of all spending going to the poorest 20 percent of the popula-

tion in 1992, a slightly lower share than in 1988.[2] There is also an urban bias in health care spending; urban Ghana received 49 percent of the health budget in 1992, up from 42 percent in 1989, despite the fact that only 33 percent of the population lives in urban areas.

Kyrgyz Republic: There is evidence of inefficiency in the Kyrgyz Republic education sector. In 1994, teaching materials accounted for less than 1 percent of all education spending. Primary education accounted for just 11 percent of education spending, compared with 67 percent for secondary education and 10 percent for higher education in the same year.[3] Wage increases in health care during 1993–95 have squeezed out other spending, such as that for operations and maintenance and immunizations. Widespread reliance on informal user charges appears to have limited the poor's access to health care.

Togo: SAF/ESAF programs do not appear to have been successful in refocusing education spending. The budgeted allocation of education expenditure between wage and nonwage outlays and among primary, secondary, and tertiary sectors remains inefficient. Wages accounted for approximately two-thirds of all education expenditure during 1990–96, while investment spending accounted for just 5 percent of these outlays. Primary education received only 41 percent of the 1995 educational budget, even though primary school enrollment accounted for 83 percent of the school population. In contrast, tertiary education received 25 percent of the budget while representing only 1 percent of the students. The share of educational expenditure allocated to nonwage items, such as teaching supplies and materials, utilities, and school infrastructure, is still too low. Since parents must pay for textbooks and supplies and for school maintenance and repair, children from poor families often do not attend school. Furthermore, repetition and dropout rates in Togo are among the highest in sub-Saharan Africa (46 percent and 7.6 percent, respectively). Only 23 percent of the population uses public health facilities, a consequence of the high cost and low quality of services. Informal user charges for medical services are common, and AIDS is spreading rapidly. Most health care resources are still concentrated in the Maritime provinces, especially the capital, Lomé, which has 35 percent of the country's population but 70 percent of the medical staff and 90 percent of the drug supply. However, there are indications that the provision of basic health care services has improved in the 1990s.

---

[1]Specific targets before 1995 were not indicated beyond an increase in spending shares. The second ESAF program, starting in 1995, has set specific targets for primary education and primary health.

[2]Note, however, that this distribution is quite progressive compared with the distribution of income.

[3]Other spending and spending not disaggregated by function account for the rest.

(although there is some evidence to suggest that the share of spending on primary education and basic health has increased in the CFA franc zone countries since 1994). In addition, in a number of countries

(Ghana, Togo, and Bolivia), wages account for as much as 95 percent of current education spending, with little left for teaching materials or other operations and maintenance outlays. The requirement for families to pay for textbooks and other supplies (Togo) limits the ability of the poorest children to attend school.

In a number of ESAF countries, the benefit incidence of education spending has been found to be regressive, with the possible exception of primary education.[54] The percentage of benefits of education expenditure accruing to the poorest quintile of the population averaged 13 percent for a sample of eight ESAF countries, compared with 32 percent for the richest quintile.[55] This finding suggests that there is substantial room for improvement in this area, for example, by increasing the share of the education budget for primary education and imposing user charges for tertiary education, or by targeting spending on poor regions.[56] A few SAF/ESAF countries were able to make progress in this direction (Ghana and Kenya).

There also appears to be considerable room for improving the productivity and benefit incidence of health care spending in ESAF countries. Health resources have been focused on in-patient care, with little spent on more cost-effective out-patient treatments (Kyrgyz Republic). There is also an inappropriate concentration of health spending by the government in higher-income regions (Bolivia and Togo). Overall, for five ESAF countries for which data are available (Côte d'Ivoire, Ghana, Kenya, Madagascar, and Vietnam), the poorest quintile receives an average of just 12 percent of the benefits of health spending, compared with 30 percent for the richest 20 percent.[57] The benefit incidence could be improved by emphasizing primary care and preventive public health services, especially in rural and poor urban areas, while spending less on curative care in large hospital settings.[58]

Poverty and Income Distribution

Spending policy affects both pretax and posttax distributions of income, and thus can potentially contribute to poverty reduction and an improved income distribution in a country. However, sustainable economic growth is ultimately the most important means of reducing poverty over the medium term.

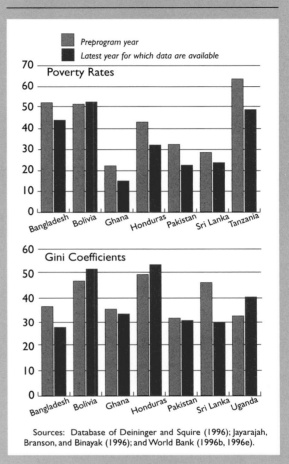

Figure 13. Poverty Rates and Gini Coefficients Under SAF/ESAF Programs

Sources: Database of Deininger and Squire (1996); Jayarajah, Branson, and Binayak (1996); and World Bank (1996b, 1996e).

Poverty rates declined by an average of about 20 percent (7.9 percentage points) during SAF/ESAF programs, based on available data for seven countries. This implies an average annual reduction of 5.3 percent.[59] The reduction for the two ESAF countries in Africa for which data are available (Tanzania and Ghana) was somewhat stronger, at 6.3 percent a year, as poverty declined sharply in both (Figure 13).[60] Significant reductions in poverty rates were experienced in Asia (Pakistan, Sri Lanka, and Bangladesh),

---

[54]See Castro-Leal, Dayton, and Demery (forthcoming).

[55]The countries are Côte d'Ivoire, Ghana, Kenya, Madagascar, Malawi, Tanzania, Lao People's Democratic Republic, and Vietnam.

[56]A number of developing countries (such as Argentina, Chile, Colombia, Malaysia, and Uruguay) have much more progressive benefit structures, with the poorest quintile capturing well over 20 percent of total benefits. For evidence on efficiency gains from targeting education spending to a poor region in Pakistan, see Alderman and others (1995).

[57]Again, this compares unfavorably with a number of other developing countries (Colombia, Malaysia, and Uruguay), in which the poor receive more than 30 percent of the health benefits.

[58]For an elaboration of options for improving the incidence of social expenditures, see, for example, Grosh (1994), Schwartz and Ter-Minassian (1995), and van de Walle (1995).

---

[59]For a larger sample of 11 countries, including countries for which the preprogram year is between 4 years and 10 years before the program, poverty declined by an average of 2.3 percent a year (see Jayarajah, Branson, and Binayak, 1996; and World Bank, 1996c, 1996d, and 1996e).

[60]The reduction in poverty in Tanzania during the ESAF may be overstated, because the preprogram year for which data are available (1983) is well before the first program (1988).

Box 10. Social Safety Nets to Cushion the Impact of Adjustment

Temporary social safety nets have been incorporated into many programs to mitigate the short-term adverse effects of price increases and reduced employment opportunities. In some cases implementation has proven difficult because of a lack of social policy instruments and poor targeting.

Bolivia: Public sector retrenchment was supported by enterprise-specific severance packages throughout the program period as well as employment creation under the aegis of the Emergency Social Fund (ESF), which was established in December 1986. ESF expenditure averaged 1.2 percent of GDP from 1988 to 1990; by end-1988, about 26,000 persons (over 1 percent of the labor force) were employed by the ESF.[1] ESAF arrangements have supported social programs that are well targeted to the poor, such as the Whole Child Development Project (PIDI), which is designed to encourage the physical, social, and cognitive development of young children and to expand mothers' knowledge of health and nutrition.

Ghana: A "special efficiency" budget was established in 1987 to cover the costs of retraining and supporting departing public sector workers. The Program to Mitigate the Social Costs of Adjustment (PAMSCAD), financed largely by the World Bank and foreign donors, was also put in place in 1988. PAMSCAD aimed at addressing the needs of vulnerable groups, including retrenched public sector workers, urban and rural poor, and particularly women and malnourished children. However, disbursements under the program were lower than expected, in part because of the complexity of the program—which included a large number of target groups and projects—the limited implementation capacity of the government, and the large number of donors. In addition, the targeting of the rural poor was seen as inadequate. In response to this, the government limited the types of projects financed under PAMSCAD and increased the emphasis on the rural poor.

Kyrgyz Republic: Progress has been made in reforming social safety nets, with measures based in part on IMF technical assistance. Generalized consumer subsidies were replaced with targeted cash compensation. Authorities consolidated three extrabudgetary funds into a single Social Fund and integrated a number of cash benefits into a single unified cash benefit (UCB), payable to individuals with incomes below the minimum wage. The means testing of the UCB was strengthened and benefits are now paid only to persons with no declared income if formally registered as unemployed. Currently, subsidies for housing, heating, and other communal services remain. Pension reform, on the other hand, has been slower than expected. Consequently, pension arrears have been mounting as generous benefits are combined with the ineffective collection of social contributions. The financial situation of the Social Fund deteriorated further in 1996, owing in part to the failure to carry out planned reforms and to an increase in pensions.

Zimbabwe: Food and health assistance, as well as retraining and microlending programs, were put in place under the ESAF program. The government also provided loans to support the formation of 13,000 new businesses by retrenched civil servants and assisted with training programs as well. Other support (outside of drought-related support), especially to cushion the adverse effects of price liberalization, appears to have been very limited.

---

[1]For more details on the ESF, see Jorgensen and others (1992). In 1991 the ESF was succeeded by the Social Investment Fund (SIF). SIF expenditures averaged 0.4 percent of GDP from 1991 through 1994.

---

while in Latin America, urban poverty increased in Bolivia and poverty at the national level declined in Honduras.[61]

Data for seven countries on income inequality indicate, on average, that the distribution of income improved during SAF/ESAF programs, with a decline in the average Gini coefficient by nearly 1 percent a year, from .41 to .39.[62] For the two ESAF countries in Africa for which data are available, income inequality increased significantly, on average, as increased inequality in Uganda more than offset a reduction in Ghana. In Asia, poverty reduction was, on average, accompanied by a more equal distribution of income, with especially sharp declines in the Gini coefficient in Bangladesh and Sri Lanka, while for the two Latin American countries, Bolivia and Honduras, income inequality increased. Similar trends can be seen in the evolution of the income share of the highest quartile to the poorest quartile. Given the small sample size, however, one should be extremely cautious in generalizing these results to other SAF/ESAF countries.

Social Safety Nets

Many countries (Albania, Guyana, Kyrgyz Republic, Mongolia, and Pakistan) have improved the efficiency of outlays on subsidies and transfers by sharply reducing generalized subsidies and increasing targeting, although data difficulties limit distin-

---

[61]The increase in poverty rates in urban areas in Bolivia was attributable to the migration of poorer rural groups to urban centers.

[62]For a larger sample of 10 countries, including 3 with earlier preprogram years, the fall in the Gini coefficient was slightly higher, at 1.1 percent per year.

guishing subsidies designed to help the poor from those designed for other policy purposes. Partly as a result of such reductions, spending on subsidies and transfers by SAF/ESAF countries declined by almost 3 percent of total spending (see also discussion above on subsidies and transfers). In a number of countries, consumer subsidies were targeted or replaced with cash compensation, and the targeting of social assistance programs strengthened. Temporary price freezes on key staples were also implemented in some countries following a major exchange rate devaluation but later removed (CFA franc zone countries). Some countries instituted new, targeted income transfer programs to assist the poor during the reform period (Mozambique and Sri Lanka).

Most countries with civil service reform programs included severance packages, as well as enhanced access to credit for microenterprises and training, often with donor financing (Bolivia, Ghana, Lao People's Democratic Republic, and Zimbabwe; see Box 10). Public works or "food for work" programs were also implemented to provide income support to the unemployed and those adversely affected by reduced employment opportunities (Bolivia, Mali, and Senegal) and for soldiers rendered unemployed by demobilization programs (Uganda). In some countries, part of the privatization proceeds was used to compensate workers who lost their jobs in privatized enterprises (Lao People's Democratic Republic and Pakistan).

Implementing social safety nets and reforming existing social programs in the context of ESAF programs have proven difficult, although countries have had some moderate success (Box 10). First, the lack of social policy instruments and weak administrative structures have hampered rapid implementation of cost-effective social safety nets, especially when the poor are dispersed across far-flung and difficult-to-reach areas (e.g., CFA franc zone countries following the 1994 devaluation). In addition, in some reforming countries, political support for implementing social safety nets targeted to the poor has at times been lacking. As a result, safety nets have not always been well targeted (Kyrgyz Republic and Sri Lanka).[63] Finally, the weakening of the revenue base for financing social benefits has limited the ability of some transition countries to provide adequate social benefits (Kyrgyz Republic).[64]

A review of actual spending on social safety nets vis-à-vis that programmed, and the impact of social safety nets in reaching the intended beneficiaries, has been hampered by inadequate data, among other things.

---

[63]The main poverty alleviation programs in Sri Lanka are the Jana Saviya, the Midday Meal, and the Food Stamp Programs. These programs were poorly targeted, and they cost some 3 percent of GDP in 1989. After reform, and without reducing assistance to the vulnerable, government expenditures on these three programs declined.

[64]See Chu and Gupta (1996).

V   Implications for Program Design

The preceding analysis shows that both revenue and expenditure policy reforms need to be viewed in the context of structural reforms more generally. But structural reforms have long gestation lags and their realization can extend beyond the program period. Thus, the structural elements of programs may need to be sufficiently front-loaded if they are to have the desired impact during the program period. The issues discussed below have potential implications for ESAF program design.

Revenue

With regard to the strategy for tax reform, priority should be given to simplifying and rationalizing tax and tariff structures and to shifting toward broad-based consumption taxes such as a modern VAT. An initial focus on the VAT is appropriate both because of the revenue consequences and because, from a sequencing perspective, the implementation of administrative reforms to support a well-functioning VAT lays the groundwork for progress with other taxes.

Although a consensus has emerged on the broad parameters of a well-designed tax system, programs have sometimes resorted to short-term, ad hoc revenue measures to meet immediate needs. Such ad hoc revenue-raising measures should, however, be viewed as temporary.

Whether a VAT contributes significantly to a more efficient tax system or to revenue mobilization or to both hinges on the VAT itself. The more disaggregated evidence suggests that those countries that enacted a VAT with a single (or, at most, two) rate(s) in the range of 15–20 percent and a minimum of exemptions typically achieved the best revenue gains, reflecting the greater buoyancy of such a tax.

Improvements in tax and customs administration are facilitated by a simplified and rationalized tax structure. An effective strategy will then reorganize the administration along functional lines, simplify procedures, pay special attention to large taxpayers, improve audits, computerize a variety of operations, and make collection and enforcement systems more effective. However, because these institutional re-

forms tend to have long gestation lags, special consideration should be given to their proper sequencing and to the possible need to front-load key measures.

The emphasis in SAF/ESAF programs on increasing the share of international trade taxes in total revenue may have been motivated, in part, by a perceived need to safeguard revenue when domestic tax policy and administration reforms ran into difficulties. Although meriting a separate inquiry, this issue underscores the need to phase tariff reforms in such a way as to provide sufficient time for domestic tax reforms to take effect.

Programs that set out specific benchmarks or prior actions on tariff policy or customs administration appear to have been associated with a stronger revenue performance compared with the overall sample. Structural benchmarks could therefore prove instrumental in ESAF reform programs. Such benchmarks should be clearly defined with monitorable actions sequenced to take into account administrative capacity.

Shortfalls in meeting annual revenue targets were most pronounced for those countries with the *lowest initial revenue effort* (based on preprogram total revenue as a percentage of GDP). However, a number of these countries significantly improved revenue performance over the program periods. This suggests that program designers should be more cognizant of the administrative limitations in implementing structural reforms when setting targets for revenue increases. Moreover, cross-country and time series evidence on revenue ratios of SAF/ESAF countries suggests that revenue ratios of more than about 20 percent of GDP are difficult to attain and, given the narrow tax bases in these countries, may be highly distortionary. Thus, while programs should emphasize revenue mobilization as key to adjustments in low-revenue countries, the balance of fiscal consolidation efforts should shift toward spending containment when the revenue ratio is more than 20 percent of GDP.

The case studies also show that sustained technical assistance is an important factor in the success of tax policy and administration reforms, especially when reinforced by strong political commitment and attention to improvements in institutional capacity. Independent external expertise also often serves as an efficient means for the spread of international good practices while providing the needed impetus for initiating and sustaining reforms.

Expenditures

Implementation of civil service reforms has been, at best, partial, with smaller-than-programmed reductions in the size of the civil service and some reliance on real wage cuts to reach wage bill targets. Accordingly, reform programs should consider incorporating explicit, monitorable quantitative targets as either structural benchmarks or performance criteria for reductions in public employment, based on actual numbers of workers rather than positions. Greater progress in this area will likely require larger input from the World Bank in support of civil service reform. In addition, programs should:

- Focus on a medium-term plan, rather than one-shot reductions, and on strengthening or creating institutions that ensure control over recruitment and the civil service payroll.
- Incorporate realistic severance packages with appropriate incentives, targeted specifically to redundant workers, including in the social sectors.
- Introduce competitive wages for highly skilled civil servants.

There is considerable scope for increasing the level, efficiency, and benefit incidence of social spending. However, program design and monitoring are constrained by the limited data on functional categories of spending and, in particular, social spending. In this respect, the following steps may be helpful in improving program design:

- Ensure that comprehensive and timely data on expenditures by function are made available.
- As data permit, expand discussion of, and trends in, social spending.
- Make social sector targets realistic, easy to monitor, and supported by underlying analysis.
- Monitor the evolution of different social indicators in ESAF countries.

The reforms of budgeting and expenditure control systems would need to incorporate the following key elements: placing greater emphasis on improving the quality of human capital, providing appropriate incentives for officials charged with implementing the reforms, and ensuring transparency and accountability. Programs should also make greater use of prior actions in this area.

In light of the adverse impact of revenue shortfalls on spending composition and the accumulation of arrears, programs may need to consider more systematically contingency measures on the expenditure side, and to specify a core budget that would be protected from cuts should the need for them arise unexpectedly. However, not all social and capital spending should necessarily be included in the core budget.

Capital expenditure targets should be based on realistic evaluations of a country's capacity to carry out capital projects, and care should be taken to protect important public investment from budget cuts.

Greater emphasis should be given to the collection and monitoring of data on government expenditures on operations and maintenance.

Greater attempts should be made also to follow up on social safety net measures, in particular to ascertain whether programs are reaching their intended beneficiaries. However, this may be difficult until country authorities improve their own efforts in this regard, especially with respect to the compilation of the relevant data.

Statistical Appendix

Table 11. Summary of Fiscal Accounts[1]
(In percent of GDP; averages of SAF/ESAF country samples)

	(1) Pre-program Year	(2) Average of Three Years Prior to Program	(3) Latest Year Actual[2]	(4)=(3)–(1) Latest Year Minus Preprogram Year	(5)=(3)–(2) Latest Year Minus Average of Three Years Prior to Program	(6) Average Program Target	(7) Average Actual During Program	(8)=(7)–(6) Average Program Actual Minus Target
Overall balance								
All sample countries								
excluding Guyana	−9.8	−9.6	−7.6	2.2	2.0	−8.9	−8.9	—
Africa	−9.2	−9.7	−7.6	1.6	2.1	−8.4	−8.7	−0.3
CFA franc countries	−8.7	−8.7	−7.5	1.2	1.2	−8.0	−7.6	0.4
Other	−9.5	−10.3	−7.6	1.9	2.6	−8.6	−9.2	−0.7
Asia	−8.8	−9.1	−6.5	2.3	2.6	−7.4	−8.1	−0.7
Western Hemisphere[3]	−5.4	−7.0	−5.4	—	1.6	−5.7	−7.5	−1.8
Transition economies	−14.7	−11.1	−9.3	5.4	1.8	−13.4	−11.2	2.2
Initial deficit[4]								
High[3]	−13.8	−13.4	−9.5	4.4	4.0	−12.1	−11.4	0.6
Medium	−7.8	−7.8	−6.4	1.4	1.5	−7.0	−7.6	−0.6
Low	−4.3	−4.1	−5.7	−1.4	−1.6	−5.5	−5.9	−0.4
Primary balance								
All sample countries								
excluding Guyana	−6.8	−6.8	−4.2	2.6	2.7	−6.0	−5.8	0.2
Of which[5]								
Africa	−6.0	−6.5	−3.9	2.1	2.6	−4.6	−4.7	−0.1
CFA franc countries	−5.0	−4.7	−4.3	0.7	0.4	−4.2	−3.6	0.6
Other	−6.6	−7.6	−3.7	2.9	4.0	−4.9	−5.4	−0.5
Transition economies	−13.8	−10.2	−8.3	7.1	3.2	−12.0	−10.1	1.9
Initial deficit[4]								
High[3]	−11.2	−10.9	−6.5	4.7	4.4	−9.2	−8.6	0.6
Medium	−4.1	−4.3	−2.7	1.5	1.8	−3.4	−3.5	−0.1
Low	−2.1	−1.8	−1.5	−0.3	−0.3	−2.9	−3.3	−0.4

Table 11 *(concluded)*

	(1) Pre-program Year	(2) Average of Three Years Prior to Program	(3) Latest Year Actual[2]	(4)=(3)−(1) Latest Year Minus Preprogram Year	(5)=(3)−(2) Latest Year Minus Average of Three Years Prior to Program	(6) Average Program Target	(7) Average Actual During Program	(8)=(7)−(6) Average Program Actual Minus Target
Current balance[6]								
All sample countries								
excluding Guyana	−1.9	−1.6	0.5	2.4	2.1	0.5	−0.1	−0.7
Africa	−1.9	−1.7	0.2	2.0	1.8	1.1	—	−1.1
CFA franc countries	−1.7	−0.9	−1.2	0.5	−0.3	0.5	−0.2	−0.7
Other	−2.0	−2.1	1.0	2.9	3.0	1.5	0.2	−1.3
Asia	1.3	1.2	0.5	−0.8	−0.7	1.7	0.7	−1.0
Western Hemisphere[3]	1.3	−1.3	4.6	3.3	5.9	1.4	0.2	−1.2
Transition economies	−5.4	−3.4	−0.2	5.3	3.2	−2.6	−1.5	1.1
Initial deficit[4]								
High[3]	−4.2	−3.3	0.5	4.7	3.8	−0.7	−0.6	0.1
Medium	0.1	−0.2	0.7	0.6	0.8	1.4	—	−1.4
Low	−0.4	−0.4	0.2	0.7	0.6	1.9	0.7	−1.2

Sources: Country authorities; and IMF staff estimates.

[1]Figures for the fiscal balance may not equal total revenue minus total expenditure as shown in Appendix Tables 13 and 23. In the latter tables, coverage is consistent with the available breakdown of expenditures and revenues. In particular, differences arise because of a broader definition of the public sector in this table (Bolivia, Guyana, and Honduras), the inclusion of election expenditures (Sierra Leone), and the exclusion of lending to public enterprises (Nepal). Differences occur also owing to the inclusion of a different "latest year" for the composition of revenues and expenditures (Bangladesh, Cambodia, Kenya, Lesotho, Uganda, and Zimbabwe) and rounding. A similar caveat applies to related figures on the current balance, primary balance, and financing.

[2]Latest year for which data are available.

[3]Average calculated without Guyana.

[4]Countries divided into high, medium, and low initial deficit based on their average deficit for the three years preceding program adoption. High-deficit countries are those with deficits greater than 10 percent of GDP; medium, 5–9.9 percent; and low, less than 5 percent.

[5]Sample size too small to include Asia and Western Hemisphere.

[6]Defined as total revenue minus current expenditure.

Table 12. Summary of Fiscal Accounts: Financing
(In percent of GDP; averages of SAF/ESAF country samples)

	(1) Pre-program Year	(2) Average of Three Years Prior to Program	(3) Latest Year Actual[1]	(4)=(3)–(1) Latest Year Minus Preprogram Year	(5)=(3)–(2) Latest Year Minus Average of Three Years Prior to Program	(6) Average Program Target	(7) Average Actual During Program	(8)=(7)–(6) Average Program Actual Minus Target
Foreign financing								
Of which:								
Foreign grants								
All sample countries								
excluding Guyana	3.0	2.7	3.0	—	0.3	4.1	3.5	–0.6
Africa	3.1	3.0	3.8	0.7	0.8	5.1	4.4	–0.7
CFA franc countries	3.4	3.6	3.5	0.1	–0.1	4.3	3.5	–0.7
Other	2.9	2.7	4.0	1.1	1.3	5.5	4.8	–0.7
Asia	3.1	3.0	1.7	–1.3	–1.2	3.0	2.8	–0.1
Western Hemisphere[2]	3.1	3.2	2.7	–0.4	–0.5	2.9	2.2	–0.7
Transition economies	2.4	1.0	1.0	–1.4	—	1.9	1.6	–0.2
Initial deficit[3]								
High[2]	3.8	3.0	3.6	–0.2	0.6	5.1	4.4	–0.7
Medium	2.7	2.9	2.7	—	–0.3	3.3	3.1	–0.2
Low	1.4	1.4	2.1	0.7	0.8	3.5	2.4	–1.1
Net foreign borrowing								
All sample countries								
excluding Guyana	3.8	3.4	3.8	—	0.4	5.8	4.7	–1.1
Africa	3.5	3.2	3.5	—	0.3	5.7	4.4	–1.3
CFA franc countries	3.0	3.1	4.7	1.6	1.5	7.1	4.8	–2.3
Other	3.7	3.2	2.8	–0.9	–0.4	4.9	4.1	–0.8
Asia	2.0	2.3	1.7	–0.2	–0.6	2.5	2.1	–0.4
Western Hemisphere[2]	3.4	4.2	3.3	–0.1	–0.9	5.0	5.5	0.4
Transition economies	6.2	4.2	6.4	0.2	2.1	8.5	7.1	–1.5
Initial deficit[3]								
High[2]	5.7	5.2	5.2	–0.5	–0.1	7.5	6.5	–0.9
Medium	2.8	2.2	1.6	–1.2	–0.7	4.2	3.2	–1.0
Low	1.1	1.1	5.2	4.2	4.2	5.2	3.5	–1.7
Domestic financing (net)[4]								
All sample countries								
excluding Guyana	3.0	3.4	1.0	–2.1	–2.4	–0.1	0.9	1.0
Africa	2.7	3.2	0.5	–2.2	–2.7	–1.1	0.1	1.2
CFA franc countries	0.6	1.2	0.2	–0.4	–1.0	–0.8	–0.2	0.6
Other	3.9	4.4	0.7	–3.2	–3.7	–1.2	0.3	1.5
Asia	3.9	3.8	3.1	–0.8	–0.7	2.0	3.1	1.2
Western Hemisphere[2]	–1.3	–0.5	–0.6	0.6	–0.2	–2.2	–0.1	2.1
Transition economies	5.8	5.6	1.9	–3.9	–3.7	3.0	2.6	–0.5
Initial deficit[3]								
High[2]	5.0	4.9	0.8	–4.2	–4.1	—	0.6	0.7
Medium	1.7	2.4	1.8	0.1	–0.5	0.1	1.4	1.3
Low	1.2	1.7	–0.5	–1.7	–2.2	–0.8	0.1	0.9
Of which:								
Financing from banking system								
All sample countries								
excluding Guyana	1.5	1.7	—	–1.5	–1.7	–0.8	–0.1	0.7
Africa	1.8	2.1	–0.3	–2.2	–2.6	–1.2	–0.3	0.9
CFA franc countries	—	0.8	0.2	0.2	–0.6	–0.5	–0.1	0.5
Other	3.0	3.0	–0.7	–3.8	–4.0	–1.6	–0.5	1.1
Asia	1.3	1.5	0.8	–0.5	–0.7	0.3	1.0	0.7
Western Hemisphere[2]	–0.4	–0.8	0.7	1.1	1.5	...	...	...
Transition economies	0.8	0.8	0.3	–0.5	–0.5	0.1	–0.1	–0.2

Table 12 *(concluded)*

	(1) Pre-program Year	(2) Average of Three Years Prior to Program	(3) Latest Year Actual[1]	(4)=(3)−(1) Latest Year Minus Preprogram Year	(5)=(3)−(2) Latest Year Minus Average of Three Years Prior to Program	(6) Average Program Target	(7) Average Actual During Program	(8)=(7)−(6) Average Program Actual Minus Target
Initial deficit[3]								
High[2]	2.7	2.5	−0.6	−3.3	−3.1	−1.6	−0.7	0.9
Medium	0.3	0.8	1.0	0.8	0.3	—	0.5	0.5
Low	1.2	1.6	−0.5	−1.8	−2.1	−0.7	—	0.7
Arrears[5]								
All sample countries excluding Guyana	—	0.2	−0.2	−0.2	−0.4	−0.8	−0.2	0.7
Africa	—	0.3	−0.3	−0.2	−0.5	−1.3	−0.2	1.1
CFA franc countries	1.7	0.7	−0.8	−2.5	−1.6	−2.6	−0.5	2.0
Other	−1.0	0.1	0.1	1.1	0.1	−0.5	−0.1	0.5
Asia	−0.1	—	—	0.1	—	—	—	—
Western Hemisphere[2]	0.2	—	—	−0.1	—	—	—	—
Transition economies	0.3	0.2	—	−0.4	−0.3	−0.1	—	—
Initial deficit[3]								
High[2]	−0.6	0.3	−0.1	0.6	−0.3	−0.5	−0.2	0.3
Medium	0.5	0.3	0.2	−0.3	—	−0.5	−0.1	0.4
Low	0.6	—	−1.2	−1.8	−1.2	−2.4	−0.1	2.3

Sources: Country authorities; and IMF staff estimates.

[1]Latest year for which data are available.

[2]Average calculated without Guyana.

[3]Countries divided into high, medium, and low initial deficit based on their average deficit in the three years preceding program adoption. High deficit countries are those with deficits greater than 10 percent of GDP; medium, 5–9.9 percent; and low, less than 5 percent.

[4]Includes privatization proceeds.

[5]Negative value indicates reduction in arrears.

Table 13. Indicators of Fiscal Adjustment: Total Revenue
(In percent of GDP)

Program Years or Years Covered	(1) Pre-program Year	(2) Average of Three Years Prior to Program	(3) Average Actual During Program	(4) Latest Year Actual[1]	(5) Average Program Target	(6)=(3)−(5) Average Program Actual Minus Target	(7)=(4)−(1) Latest Year Minus Preprogram Year	(8)=(4)−(2) Latest Year Minus Average of Three Years Prior to Program
Albania 1993–95	24.7	34.3	27.5	26.9	24.5	3.0	2.2	-7.4
Bangladesh 1986/87–1988/89, 1990/91–1992/93	8.8	8.4	9.5	10.8	10.0	-0.5	2.1	2.4
Benin 1989–91, 1993–95	12.7	12.9	11.8	14.4	11.6	0.2	1.7	1.5
Bolivia 1987–92, 1994–95	19.9	15.4	21.1	22.9	20.8	0.3	3.0	7.6
Burkina Faso 1991, 1993–95	12.3	11.4	12.3	12.2	12.4	-0.2	-0.2	0.8
Burundi 1986–89, 1991–93	14.2	13.6	16.5	18.8	18.2	-1.8	4.6	5.2
Cambodia 1994–95	5.4	5.3	9.3	8.9	8.6	0.6	3.6	3.6
Côte d'Ivoire 1994–95	17.6	18.9	21.2	21.9	21.2	—	4.3	3.0
Equatorial Guinea 1989, 1991, 1993–94	18.0	19.7	18.7	14.9	19.9	-1.2	-3.0	-4.7
Gambia, The 1986/87–1991/92	24.3	22.4	26.3	19.4	27.1	-0.7	-5.0	-3.0
Ghana 1987–92, 1995	13.6	11.1	14.3	22.3	15.0	-0.7	8.7	11.2
Guinea 1987–89, 1991–92, 1994–95	13.1	13.1	13.5	11.0	12.2	1.3	-2.1	-2.1
Guyana 1990–93, 1994–95	28.8	34.3	32.8	33.5	32.5	0.3	4.8	-0.8
Honduras 1992–93, 1995	17.5	16.2	18.0	18.1	17.4	0.6	0.6	1.9
Kenya 1987/88–1991/92, 1993/94–1994/95	22.6	22.3	24.3	29.0	23.9	0.3	6.5	6.8
Kyrgyz Republic 1994–95	15.2	22.2	16.8	15.3	23.9	-7.1	0.1	-6.9
Lao People's Dem. Rep. 1989/90–1995/96	12.5	13.9	10.4	14.9	11.8	-1.4	2.5	1.0
Lesotho 1988/89–1994/95	19.3	21.1	26.0	30.4	25.7	0.3	11.1	9.2
Madagascar 1987–91	9.6	10.7	9.7	8.3	14.3	-4.5	-1.2	-2.4
Malawi 1988/89–1993/94, 1995/96	20.7	21.3	19.2	17.6	19.0	0.2	-3.1	-3.7
Mali 1988–90, 1992–95	15.1	16.0	14.8	14.4	15.0	-0.2	-0.7	-1.6
Mauritania 1986–87, 1989, 1992–95	23.7	23.2	23.2	20.7	24.5	-1.2	-3.0	-2.5
Mongolia 1993–95	27.3	41.7	31.7	33.6	28.2	3.5	6.2	-8.2
Mozambique 1987–94	13.3	15.6	20.3	18.3	21.6	-1.3	5.0	2.7
Nepal 1987/88–1989/90, 1992/93–1994/95	9.8	9.4	9.6	10.5	10.4	-0.8	0.7	1.1
Nicaragua 1994	20.1	20.0	20.3	21.7	21.1	-0.8	1.7	1.7
Niger 1986–88, 1990	11.4	11.1	10.6	7.5	11.5	-0.8	-4.0	-3.6
Pakistan 1988/89–1989/90, 1991/92, 1993/94–1994/95	17.3	17.6	17.7	17.0	19.4	-1.6	-0.3	-0.7
Senegal 1986–91, 1994–95	17.6	18.9	17.2	15.1	17.4	-0.2	-2.5	-3.8
Sierra Leone 1986/87, 1993/94–1995/96	5.4	6.2	10.6	10.0	11.9	-1.3	4.6	3.8
Sri Lanka 1988–94	21.4	21.5	20.1	20.6	20.7	-0.6	-0.8	-0.9
Tanzania 1987/88–1992/93	16.1	16.7	20.0	15.0	21.7	-1.8	-1.1	-1.7
Togo 1988–90, 1994	23.7	25.3	20.4	12.5	20.7	-0.3	-11.2	-12.9
Uganda 1987/88–1992/93, 1994/95	4.9	7.3	7.3	10.9	8.1	-0.8	6.0	3.6
Vietnam 1994–95	21.6	17.7	23.4	23.3	23.2	0.2	1.7	5.6
Zimbabwe 1992/93–1995/96	36.0	34.0	29.6	28.5	30.0	-0.4	-7.5	-5.5
Unweighted average	17.1	18.1	18.2	18.1	18.8	-0.5	1.0	—
Median	17.4	17.2	18.4	17.3	19.6	-1.3	-0.1	0.1

Sources: Country authorities; and IMF staff estimates.
[1] Latest year for which data are available.

Table 14. Indicators of Fiscal Adjustment: Tax Revenue
(In percent of GDP)

	Program Years or Years Covered	(1) Preprogram Year	(2) Average of Three Years Prior to Program	(3) Average Actual During Program	(4) Latest Year Actual[1]	(5) Average Program Target	(6)=(3)–(5) Average Program Actual Minus Target	(7)=(4)–(1) Latest Year Minus Preprogram Year	(8)=(4)–(2) Latest Year Minus Average of Three Years Prior to Program
Albania	1993–95	17.2	28.7	20.5	21.0	21.6	–1.1	3.8	–7.7
Bangladesh	1986/87–1988/89, 1990/91–1992/93	7.1	7.0	7.7	8.7	8.3	–0.6	1.6	1.7
Benin	1989–91, 1993–95	9.9	10.7	9.6	11.9	9.8	–0.2	2.0	1.1
Bolivia	1987–92, 1994–95	3.9	3.0	11.8	19.5	11.7	0.1	15.6	16.6
Burkina Faso	1991, 1993–95	10.2	9.6	10.1	11.0	10.7	–0.6	0.8	1.3
Burundi	1986–89, 1991–93	13.1	12.6	14.3	17.8	16.1	–1.8	4.7	5.2
Cambodia	1994–95	4.2	3.6	6.1	6.2	5.8	0.2	2.0	2.6
Côte d'Ivoire	1994–95	14.8	16.2	17.1	17.8	17.2	–0.1	3.1	1.6
Equatorial Guinea	1989, 1991, 1993–94	14.1	14.2	13.0	9.3	13.0	—	–4.8	–4.9
Gambia, The	1986/87–1991/92	22.4	20.5	23.1	16.9	24.2	–1.0	–5.5	–3.5
Ghana	1987–92, 1995	12.2	9.4	12.2	15.0	13.4	–1.1	2.8	5.6
Guinea	1987–89, 1991–92, 1994–95	13.1	13.1	12.6	10.3	8.0	4.6	–2.8	–2.8
Guyana	1990–93, 1994–95	25.2	30.9	...	31.6	...	...	6.4	0.7
Honduras	1992–93, 1995	16.0	14.4	16.6	17.3	16.0	0.6	1.3	2.9
Kenya	1987/88–1991/92, 1993/94–1994/95	20.0	19.5	24.1	25.8	20.1	4.1	5.9	6.4
Kyrgyz Republic	1994–95	13.5	15.0	13.5	13.6	18.6	–5.1	0.1	–1.4
Lao People's Dem. Rep.	1989/90–1995/96	9.4	4.1	7.3	12.2	9.3	–2.1	2.8	8.1
Lesotho	1988/89–1994/95	16.8	18.5	18.3	25.5	20.2	–1.8	8.7	7.0
Madagascar	1987–91	9.3	10.3	9.3	8.1	12.8	–3.5	–1.2	–2.2
Malawi	1988/89–1993/94, 1995/96	16.0	17.1	16.4	15.3	16.2	0.2	–0.7	–1.8
Mali	1988–90, 1992–95	9.6	10.5	10.0	10.7	10.9	–0.9	1.1	0.2
Mauritania	1986–87, 1989, 1992–95	19.7	18.8	17.8	17.0	19.6	–1.8	–2.7	–1.8
Mongolia	1993–95	23.2	32.4	26.2	26.2	25.2	1.0	3.0	–6.2
Mozambique	1987–94	9.4	11.2	17.8	16.7	19.4	–1.6	7.3	5.5
Nepal	1987/88–1989/90, 1992/93–1994/95	7.4	7.4	...	8.9	...	...	1.5	1.5
Nicaragua	1994	18.5	18.5	19.1	20.3	19.8	–0.7	1.8	1.8
Niger	1986–88, 1990	9.6	9.4	8.3	6.8	9.3	–1.0	–2.8	–2.6
Pakistan	1988/89–1989/90, 1991/92, 1993/94–1994/95	13.8	14.1	13.8	13.8	15.0	–1.2	—	–0.3
Senegal	1986–91, 1994–95	14.9	17.1	14.4	13.6	14.9	–0.5	–1.3	–3.5
Sierra Leone	1986/87, 1993/94–1995/96	5.1	5.9	10.3	9.9	11.8	–1.4	4.8	4.0
Sri Lanka	1988–94	17.9	18.0	17.8	17.9	18.3	–0.4	—	–0.1
Tanzania	1987/88–1992/93	15.1	15.7	17.7	12.8	19.9	–2.3	–2.3	–2.9
Togo	1988–90, 1994	19.4	20.3	17.2	11.3	16.5	0.7	–8.1	–9.0
Uganda	1987/88–1992/93, 1994/95	4.1	6.9	6.9	10.6	7.4	–0.6	6.5	3.7
Vietnam	1994–95	17.4	13.7	19.2	19.7	20.8	–1.6	2.3	6.0
Zimbabwe	1992/93–1995/96	33.1	30.8	25.9	24.3	26.4	–0.5	–8.8	–6.5
Unweighted average		14.1	14.7	14.9	15.4	15.5	–0.6	1.4	0.7
Median		14.0	14.2	14.4	14.4	16.1	–1.7	0.4	0.2

Sources: Country authorities; and IMF staff estimates.
[1] Latest year for which data are available.

Table 15. Indicators of Fiscal Adjustment: Taxes on Domestic Goods and Services
(In percent of GDP)

Program Years or Years Covered	(1) Pre-program Year	(2) Average of Three Years Prior to Program	(3) Average Actual During Program	(4) Latest Year Actual[1]	(5) Average Program Target	(6)=(3)–(5) Average Program Actual Minus Target	(7)=(4)–(1) Latest Year Minus Preprogram Year	(8)=(4)–(2) Latest Year Minus Average of Three Years Prior to Program
Albania	1993–95	7.2	14.8	8.3	8.4	8.0	0.4	1.3	–6.3
Bangladesh	1986/87–1988/89, 1990/91–1992/93	2.6	2.6	...	4.1	...	...	1.5	1.4
Benin	1989–91, 1993–95	1.3	1.3	...	1.9	...	...	0.6	0.6
Bolivia	1987–92, 1994–95	...	...	10.7	11.3	10.2	0.5	11.3	11.3
Burkina Faso	1991, 1993–95	2.4	2.3	2.0	2.0	2.3	–0.3	–0.4	–0.3
Burundi	1986–89, 1991–93	4.9	5.1	5.8	7.1	6.1	–0.3	2.1	2.0
Cambodia	1994–95	0.3	0.3	...	1.2	...	...	0.9	0.9
Côte d'Ivoire	1994–95	8.6	9.0	7.3	7.3	7.4	–0.1	–1.3	–1.7
Equatorial Guinea	1989, 1991, 1993–94	6.1	5.5	3.7	3.6	3.8	–0.1	–2.5	–1.9
Gambia, The	1986/87–1991/92	1.5	1.6	8.4	5.4	7.1	1.3	3.8	3.8
Ghana	1987–92, 1995	4.3	3.1	5.3	6.6	4.8	0.5	2.4	3.6
Guinea	1987–89, 1991–92, 1994–95	...	...	3.1	4.7	3.1	–0.1	...	...
Guyana	1990–93, 1994–95	8.1	10.2	...	11.4	...	...	3.3	1.2
Honduras	1992–93, 1995	5.8	5.2	6.4	6.8	6.7	–0.3	1.1	1.6
Kenya	1987/88–1991/92, 1993/94–1994/95	8.9	8.4	10.6	12.0	9.7	0.9	3.1	3.6
Kyrgyz Republic	1994–95	5.3	7.2	6.8	7.4	8.6	–1.8	2.1	0.2
Lao People's Dem. Rep.	1989/90–1995/96	3.2	1.5	1.9	3.0	1.8	0.1	–0.2	1.5
Lesotho	1988/89–1994/95	4.2	3.8	4.4	4.0	4.0	0.5	–0.2	0.2
Madagascar	1987–91	3.1	3.3	...	2.1	...	...	–0.9	–1.2
Malawi	1988/89–1993/94, 1995/96	6.4	6.4	...	8.0	...	...	1.6	1.6
Mali	1988–90, 1992–95	1.6	1.7	...	1.3	...	...	–0.3	–0.4
Mauritania	1986–87, 1989, 1992–95	3.7	3.3	3.4	5.4	3.6	–0.2	1.7	2.1
Mongolia	1993–95	6.4	7.4	4.6	4.2	4.5	0.1	–2.2	–3.1
Mozambique	1987–94	5.4	6.2	9.2	8.7	10.2	–1.0	3.3	2.6
Nepal	1987/88–1989/90, 1992/93–1994/95	3.6	3.6	...	4.0	...	...	0.4	0.3
Nicaragua	1994	12.0	11.6	...	12.8	...	...	0.8	1.3
Niger	1986–88, 1990	4.6	4.6	3.3	1.3	2.2	1.2	–3.3	–3.3
Pakistan	1988/89–1989/90, 1991/92, 1993/94–1994/95	5.8	5.9	5.9	5.8	6.6	–0.7	—	–0.1
Senegal	1986–91, 1994–95	4.7	5.3	...	3.4	...	...	–1.2	–1.8
Sierra Leone	1986/87, 1993/94–1995/96	1.1	1.5	3.4	3.0	3.9	–0.4	1.9	1.6
Sri Lanka	1988–94	8.0	8.1	...	10.7	...	...	2.7	2.6
Tanzania	1987/88–1992/93	8.3	8.8	7.4	3.5	8.4	–1.0	–4.8	–5.3
Togo	1988–90, 1994	2.6	2.3	1.8	1.0	2.0	–0.2	–1.6	–1.3
Uganda	1987/88–1992/93, 1994/95	1.4	1.7	...	4.2	...	...	2.7	2.5
Vietnam	1994–95	6.0	5.4	...	5.9	...	...	–0.1	0.5
Zimbabwe	1992/93–1995/96	8.2	7.9	6.2	6.6	6.7	–0.5	–1.6	–1.3
Unweighted average		4.9	5.2	5.7	5.6	5.7	–0.1	0.8	0.5
Median		4.8	5.1	5.8	5.0	6.1	–0.3	0.2	–0.1

Sources: Country authorities; and IMF staff estimates.
[1]Latest year for which data are available.

Table 16. Indicators of Fiscal Adjustment: Taxes on Income, Profits, and Capital Gains
(In percent of GDP)

	Program Years or Years Covered	(1) Pre-program Year	(2) Average of Three Years Prior to Program	(3) Average Actual During Program	(4) Latest Year Actual[1]	(5) Average Program Target	(6)=(3)−(5) Average Program Actual Minus Target	(7)=(4)−(1) Latest Year Minus Preprogram Year	(8)=(4)−(2) Latest Year Average Minus Average of Three Years Prior to Program
Albania	1993–95	6.6	12.6	6.7	6.5	10.3	−3.6	−0.1	−6.1
Bangladesh	1986/87–1988/89, 1990/91–1992/93	1.0	0.9	...	1.1	...	...	0.2	0.2
Benin	1989–91, 1993–95	2.9	3.1	...	3.9	...	...	1.0	0.7
Bolivia	1987–92, 1994–95	...	...	6.8	6.5	7.1	−0.3	...	...
Burkina Faso	1991, 1993–95	2.9	2.5	2.6	2.7	2.4	0.2	−0.2	0.2
Burundi	1986–89, 1991–93	2.9	3.2	3.6	3.7	3.3	0.3	0.8	0.5
Cambodia	1994–95	1.1	1.0	...	0.3	...	...	−0.8	−0.7
Côte d'Ivoire	1994–95	3.4	3.9	3.5	4.0	3.2	0.3	0.6	0.2
Equatorial Guinea	1989, 1991, 1993–94	1.3	0.9	0.6	0.4	0.3	0.2	−0.8	−0.5
Gambia, The	1986/87–1991/92	3.7	3.4	3.3	4.0	3.1	0.2	0.2	0.6
Ghana	1987–92, 1995	2.8	2.1	3.0	3.6	3.1	−0.1	0.9	1.5
Guinea	1987–89, 1991–92, 1994–95	11.2	11.2	8.1	4.0	0.6	7.5	−7.2	−7.2
Guyana	1990–93, 1994–95	10.6	13.0	...	12.9	...	...	2.3	−0.1
Honduras	1992–93, 1995	4.0	3.6	4.9	4.8	4.2	0.7	0.8	1.2
Kenya	1987/88–1991/92, 1993/94–1994/95	6.2	6.4	9.6	9.6	6.4	3.2	3.4	3.2
Kyrgyz Republic	1994–95	5.2	6.2	4.8	4.1	6.9	−2.1	−1.1	−2.1
Lao People's Dem. Rep.	1989/90–1995/96	3.3	1.4	1.6	2.7	1.3	0.3	−0.6	1.3
Lesotho	1988/89–1994/95	2.4	2.6	3.8	5.0	3.5	0.3	2.6	2.4
Madagascar	1987–91	1.9	2.2	...	1.3	...	...	−0.6	−0.9
Malawi	1988/89–1993/94, 1995/96	6.4	6.9	...	5.3	...	...	−1.1	−1.6
Mali	1988–90, 1992–95	1.7	1.9	...	2.6	...	...	0.9	0.8
Mauritania	1986–87, 1989, 1992–95	5.6	5.9	6.6	6.1	7.0	−0.5	0.5	0.2
Mongolia	1993–95	13.6	17.9	15.7	17.4	10.4	5.4	3.8	−0.5
Mozambique	1987–94	2.6	3.2	3.8	3.6	3.2	0.6	1.0	0.4
Nepal	1987/88–1989/90, 1992/93–1994/95	1.3	1.3	...	1.7	1.8	...	0.4	0.4
Nicaragua	1994	2.4	3.1	...	2.8	...	...	0.3	−0.3
Niger	1986–88, 1990	2.7	2.5	2.7	2.3	2.5	0.1	−0.3	−0.2
Pakistan	1988/89–1989/90, 1991/92, 1993/94–1994/95	1.8	1.9	2.5	3.4	2.5	—	1.5	1.4
Senegal	1986–91, 1994–95	4.2	4.6	...	3.5	...	...	−0.7	−1.1
Sierra Leone	1986/87, 1993/94–1995/96	1.4	1.7	1.9	1.4	1.8	0.1	...	−0.3
Sri Lanka	1988–94	3.3	3.4	...	3.4	...	...	0.1	—
Tanzania	1987/88–1992/93	3.6	4.3	4.7	3.8	4.3	0.5	0.1	−0.5
Togo	1988–90, 1994	7.6	8.5	6.9	5.0	3.8	3.1	−2.6	−3.5
Uganda	1987/88–1992/93, 1994/95	0.5	0.5	...	1.6	...	...	1.1	1.1
Vietnam	1994–95	4.9	3.7	...	5.3	...	...	0.4	1.6
Zimbabwe	1992/93–1995/96	15.2	15.5	13.9	12.3	13.6	0.3	−3.0	−3.2
Unweighted average		4.4	4.8	5.3	4.5	4.6	0.7	0.1	−0.3
Median		3.3	3.2	3.8	3.7	3.3	0.5	0.4	0.5

Sources: Country authorities; and IMF staff estimates.
[1] Latest year for which data are available.

Table 17. Indicators of Fiscal Adjustment: Taxes on International Trade
(In percent of GDP)

Program Years or Years Covered	(1) Pre-program Year	(2) Average of Three Years Prior to Program	(3) Average Actual During Program	(4) Latest Year Actual[1]	(5) Average Program Target	(6)=(3)–(5) Average Program Actual Minus Target	(7)=(4)–(1) Latest Year Minus Preprogram Year	(8)=(4)–(2) Latest Year Average Minus Average of Three Years Prior to Program
Albania 1993–95	3.0	1.8	3.5	3.8	3.8	–0.3	0.8	2.0
Bangladesh 1986/87–1988/89, 1990/91–1992/93	2.8	2.7	...	2.7	...	...	—	—
Benin 1989–91, 1993–95	5.4	6.0	5.4	5.8	5.6	–0.1	0.4	–0.2
Bolivia 1987–92, 1994–95	...	...	1.6	1.6	1.6	—	1.6	1.6
Burkina Faso 1991, 1993–95	4.7	4.7	5.4	6.2	5.7	–0.3	1.4	1.4
Burundi 1986–89, 1991–93	5.3	4.4	4.6	7.0	6.3	–1.7	1.7	2.6
Cambodia 1994–95	2.9	2.6	4.5	4.5	4.3	0.2	1.5	1.9
Côte d'Ivoire 1994–95	2.7	3.3	6.2	6.4	6.6	–0.4	3.6	3.0
Equatorial Guinea 1989, 1991, 1993–94	6.8	7.7	5.5	4.4	7.2	–1.7	–2.4	–3.3
Gambia, The 1986/87–1991/92	17.1	15.5	11.4	7.6	13.0	–1.6	–9.6	–7.9
Ghana 1987–92, 1995	5.1	4.2	3.9	4.7	5.5	–1.6	–0.4	0.6
Guinea 1987–89, 1991–92, 1994–95	0.8	0.8	1.4	1.6	1.5	–0.1	0.8	0.8
Guyana 1990–93, 1994–95	3.9	4.1	...	4.7	...	...	0.8	0.6
Honduras 1992–93, 1995	5.8	5.3	5.0	4.7	4.8	0.1	–1.1	–0.6
Kenya 1987/88–1991/92, 1993/94–1994/95	4.5	4.4	3.9	4.2	4.0	–0.1	–0.3	–0.2
Kyrgyz Republic 1994–95	0.5	0.5	0.6	0.8	0.8	–0.2	0.3	0.3
Lao People's Dem. Rep. 1989/90–1995/96	2.8	1.1	2.3	3.5	3.0	–0.7	0.7	2.4
Lesotho 1988/89–1994/95	10.2	12.1	14.3	16.4	14.6	–0.3	6.2	4.2
Madagascar 1987–91	4.2	4.7	...	4.6	...	...	0.4	–0.1
Malawi 1988/89–1993/94, 1995/96	3.1	3.7	7.3	7.3	8.1	–0.8	4.2	3.6
Mali 1988–90, 1992–95	4.0	4.5	5.9	5.9	6.1	–0.2	1.9	1.4
Mauritania 1986–87, 1989, 1992–95	9.0	8.6	...	5.4	...	...	–3.6	–3.2
Mongolia 1993–95	3.3	7.1	5.2	4.6	6.0	–0.8	1.4	–2.5
Mozambique 1987–94	0.9	1.2	4.3	4.4	5.6	–1.3	3.5	3.2
Nepal 1987/88–1989/90, 1992/93–1994/95	2.5	2.5	...	3.2	...	...	0.6	0.6
Nicaragua 1994	4.0	3.8	...	4.7	...	...	0.7	0.9
Niger 1986–88, 1990	2.2	2.3	2.2	3.1	4.2	–2.0	0.9	0.9
Pakistan 1988/89–1989/90, 1991/92, 1993/94–1994/95	5.6	5.7	4.9	4.2	5.2	–0.3	–1.5	–1.5
Senegal 1986–91, 1994–95	5.9	7.0	...	6.4	...	...	0.5	–0.6
Sierra Leone 1986/87, 1993/94–1995/96	2.5	2.6	4.8	4.9	5.7	–0.9	2.4	2.3
Sri Lanka 1988–94	6.6	6.5	...	3.7	...	...	–2.9	–2.8
Tanzania 1987/88–1992/93	2.1	1.6	3.8	4.1	5.6	–1.8	2.0	2.5
Togo 1988–90, 1994	8.4	8.8	6.8	5.1	6.9	—	–3.4	–3.7
Uganda 1987/88–1992/93, 1994/95	2.2	4.8	...	4.3	...	...	2.0	–0.5
Vietnam 1994–95	4.3	2.6	...	6.6	...	...	2.3	4.0
Zimbabwe 1992/93–1995/96	9.0	6.8	5.2	4.6	5.6	–0.4	–4.4	–2.2
Unweighted average	4.7	4.7	5.0	4.9	5.7	–0.7	0.4	0.3
Median	4.0	4.4	4.8	4.6	5.6	–0.7	0.6	0.2

Sources: Country authorities; and IMF staff estimates.

[1]Latest year for which data are available.

Table 18. Indicators of Fiscal Adjustment: Nontax Revenue
(In percent of GDP)

	Program Years or Years Covered	(1) Pre-program Year	(2) Average of Three Years Prior to Program	(3) Average Actual During Program	(4) Latest Year Actual[1]	(5) Average Program Target	(6)=(3)-(5) Average Program Actual Minus Target	(7)=(4)-(1) Latest Year Minus Preprogram Year	(8)=(4)-(2) Latest Year Minus Average of Three Years Prior to Program
Albania	1993–95	7.5	5.6	7.0	5.9	2.8	4.3	-1.6	0.3
Bangladesh	1986/87–1988/89, 1990/91–1992/93	1.7	1.4	1.9	2.1	1.9	—	0.5	0.7
Benin	1989–91, 1993–95	2.9	2.2	2.2	2.5	1.7	0.4	-0.3	0.3
Bolivia	1987–92, 1994–95	16.0	12.4	9.3	3.4	9.2	0.1	-12.6	-9.0
Burkina Faso	1991, 1993–95	2.2	1.8	2.2	1.2	1.1	1.1	-1.0	-0.5
Burundi	1986–89, 1991–93	1.1	1.0	2.1	1.0	2.1	—	—	0.1
Cambodia	1994–95	1.2	1.7	3.2	2.7	2.8	0.4	1.6	1.0
Côte d'Ivoire	1994–95	2.8	2.7	4.1	4.1	4.1	—	1.3	1.4
Equatorial Guinea	1989, 1991, 1993–94	3.9	5.5	5.8	5.6	7.0	-1.2	1.8	0.1
Gambia, The	1986/87–1991/92	1.9	1.9	2.1	2.5	1.8	0.3	0.5	0.6
Ghana	1987–92, 1995	1.4	1.7	2.1	7.3	1.7	0.4	5.9	5.6
Guinea	1987–89, 1991–92, 1994–95	—	—	0.9	0.7	0.6	0.3	0.7	0.7
Guyana	1990–93, 1994–95	3.5	3.4	...	1.9	...	...	-1.6	-1.4
Honduras	1992–93, 1995	1.5	1.8	1.4	0.8	0.9	0.5	-0.7	-1.0
Kenya	1987/88–1991/92, 1993/94–1994/95	2.6	2.8	2.7	3.2	3.2	-0.5	0.6	0.4
Kyrgyz Republic	1994–95	1.5	7.1	2.9	1.4	5.1	-2.2	-0.1	-5.7
Lao People's Dem. Rep.	1989/90–1995/96	3.1	9.8	3.7	2.8	2.5	1.2	-0.3	-7.1
Lesotho	1988/89–1994/95	2.5	2.6	3.4	4.8	3.2	0.3	2.4	2.2
Madagascar	1987–91	0.3	0.4	0.4	0.2	1.5	-1.1	—	-0.2
Malawi	1988/89–1993/94, 1995/96	4.7	4.2	2.8	2.3	2.7	0.1	-2.4	-1.9
Mali	1988–90, 1992–95	5.5	5.5	4.8	3.7	1.3	3.4	-1.8	-1.8
Mauritania	1986–87, 1989, 1992–95	4.0	4.4	5.4	3.7	4.4	1.0	-0.2	-0.7
Mongolia	1993–95	4.1	9.3	5.5	7.4	2.0	3.5	3.3	-1.9
Mozambique	1987–94	3.9	4.4	2.5	1.6	2.2	0.3	-2.3	-2.8
Nepal	1987/88–1989/90, 1992/93–1994/95	2.4	1.9	...	1.6	...	...	-0.8	-0.3
Nicaragua	1994	1.6	1.5	1.2	1.4	1.3	-0.1	-0.2	-0.1
Niger	1986–88, 1990	1.8	1.6	2.4	0.7	1.9	0.5	-1.2	-1.0
Pakistan	1988/89–1989/90, 1991/92, 1993/94–1994/95	3.5	3.5	3.9	3.2	4.7	-0.8	-0.3	-0.3
Senegal	1986–91, 1994–95	2.7	1.8	2.9	1.5	2.5	0.4	-1.2	-0.3
Sierra Leone	1986/87, 1993/94–1995/96	0.3	0.4	0.2	0.2	0.1	0.1	-0.2	-0.2
Sri Lanka	1988–94	3.5	3.5	2.3	2.7	2.2	—	-0.8	-0.8
Tanzania	1987/88–1992/93	1.0	1.0	2.3	2.2	1.7	0.6	1.2	1.2
Togo	1988–90, 1994	4.3	5.0	3.2	1.2	3.2	—	-3.1	-3.9
Uganda	1987/88–1992/93, 1994/95	0.8	0.3	0.4	0.3	0.6	-0.2	-0.5	—
Vietnam	1994–95	4.2	4.0	4.3	3.6	4.0	0.3	-0.6	-0.4
Zimbabwe	1992/93–1995/96	2.9	3.2	3.7	4.2	3.6	0.1	1.3	1.0
Unweighted average		3.0	3.4	3.1	2.7	2.7	0.4	-0.4	-0.7
Median		2.6	2.7	2.8	2.4	2.2	0.5	-0.3	-0.3

Sources: Country authorities; and IMF staff estimates.

[1] Latest year for which data are available.

Table 19. Revenue: Summary of Program Targets by Initial Revenue Ratio[1]

	Average of Three Years Prior to Program	Pre-program Year	Average Program Target[2]	Target ≥ Preprogram Actual	Target < Preprogram Actual	Number of Countries[3]
	In percent of GDP			*Percent of countries*		
Countries with low initial revenue effort						
Total revenue	7.9	7.3	10.5	100	—	6
Tax revenue	6.9	6.2	9.2	100	—	5
Taxes on domestic goods and services	2.1	2.0	3.9	100	—	1
Taxes on income, profits, and capital gains	1.3	1.2	1.8	100	—	1
Taxes on international trade	3.3	2.9	5.0	100	—	2
Nontax revenue	1.0	1.1	1.4	60	40	5
Countries with medium initial revenue effort						
Total revenue	15.9	15.4	17.6	67	33	18
Tax revenue	12.2	12.2	14.1	72	28	18
Taxes on domestic goods and services	4.8	4.8	5.7	54	46	13
Taxes on income, profits, and capital gains	3.5	3.5	3.2	57	43	14
Taxes on international trade	4.3	4.2	5.2	73	27	15
Nontax revenue	3.7	3.2	3.0	56	44	18
Countries with high initial revenue effort						
Total revenue	26.5	24.6	24.6	58	42	12
Tax revenue	22.4	20.8	20.8	67	25	11
Taxes on domestic goods and services	7.3	6.6	5.9	57	43	7
Taxes on income, profits, and capital gains	8.4	7.2	7.8	43	57	7
Taxes on international trade	6.1	6.4	6.5	33	67	6
Nontax revenue	4.0	3.7	2.8	25	75	11

Sources: Country authorities; and IMF staff estimates.

[1]Results for the total SAF/ESAF sample are reported in Table 1. Initial revenue efforts (ratios) were arbitrarily based on total revenue as a percentage of GDP, classified as follows: *low,* between 5 and 9.9 percent; *medium,* between 10 and 19.9 percent; and *high,* more than 20 percent.

[2]The components do not sum to the total because of differing sample sizes.

[3]Number of countries in the SAF/ESAF sample for which data are available for a given revenue category. If the sample size varies for different columns, the maximum number is given.

Table 20. Revenue: Summary of Program Targets by Region[1]

	Average of Three Years Prior to Program	Pre-program Year	Average Program Target[2]	Target ≥ Preprogram Actual	Target < Preprogram Actual	Number of Countries[3]
	⟵———— In percent of GDP ————⟶			Percent of countries		
Africa CFA franc zone countries						
Total revenue	16.8	16.1	16.2	50	50	8
Tax revenue	13.5	12.8	12.8	50	50	8
Taxes on domestic goods and services	4.0	4.0	3.5	—	100	5
Taxes on income, profits, and capital gains	3.5	3.3	2.4	—	100	5
Taxes on international trade	5.5	5.0	6.0	67	33	6
Nontax revenue	3.3	3.3	2.8	38	63	8
Africa non-CFA franc zone countries						
Total revenue	17.0	16.9	19.5	79	21	14
Tax revenue	15.0	15.0	16.8	79	21	14
Taxes on domestic goods and services	4.7	4.7	6.1	60	40	10
Taxes on income, profits, and capital gains	4.9	4.8	4.6	73	27	11
Taxes on international trade	5.4	5.4	7.0	67	33	9
Nontax revenue	2.0	2.0	2.1	64	36	14
Asian countries						
Total revenue	14.2	14.3	15.1	75	25	4
Tax revenue	11.6	11.6	13.8	100	—	3
Taxes on domestic goods and services	5.1	5.0	6.6	100	—	1
Taxes on income, profits, and capital gains	1.9	1.9	2.5	100	—	1
Taxes on international trade	4.4	4.4	5.2	—	100	1
Nontax revenue	2.6	2.8	2.9	67	33	3
Western Hemisphere countries						
Total revenue	21.5	21.6	22.9	75	25	4
Tax revenue	16.7	15.9	15.8	100	—	3
Taxes on domestic goods and services	9.0	8.6	8.4	100	—	1
Taxes on income, profits, and capital gains	6.6	5.7	5.6	100	—	1
Taxes on international trade	4.4	4.6	3.2	—	100	1
Nontax revenue	4.8	5.6	3.8	—	100	3
Transition economies						
Total revenue	22.5	17.8	20.0	50	50	6
Tax revenue	16.3	14.1	16.9	67	33	6
Taxes on domestic goods and services	6.1	4.7	5.7	50	50	4
Taxes on income, profits, and capital gains	7.1	5.8	7.2	25	75	4
Taxes on international trade	2.5	2.8	3.6	100	—	5
Nontax revenue	6.2	3.6	3.2	17	83	6

Sources: Country authorities; and IMF staff estimates.

[1]Results for the total SAF/ESAF sample are reported in Table 1.

[2]The components do not sum to the total because of differing sample sizes.

[3]Number of countries in the SAF/ESAF sample for which data are available for a given revenue category. If the sample size varies for different columns, the maximum number is given.

Table 21. Revenue: Summary of Program Implementation by Region[1]

	Average Program Target	Average Actual During Program	Program Actual Minus Target[2]	Actual ≥ Target	Actual < Target	Number of Countries[3]	Preprogram Year	Latest Year[4]	Latest Year Minus Preprogram Year
	In percent of GDP			*Percent of countries*			*In percent of GDP*		
Africa CFA franc zone countries									
Total revenue	16.2	15.9	-0.3	13	88	8	16.1	14.1	-1.9
Tax revenue	12.8	12.5	-0.3	13	88	8	12.8	11.5	-1.2
Taxes on domestic goods and services	3.5	3.6	0.1	20	80	5	4.0	2.7	-1.3
Taxes on income, profits, and capital gains	2.4	3.3	0.8	100	—	5	3.3	3.1	-0.3
Taxes on international trade	6.0	5.3	-0.8	—	100	6	5.0	5.4	0.4
Nontax revenue	2.8	3.4	0.6	75	25	8	3.3	2.6	-0.7
Africa non-CFA franc zone countries									
Total revenue	19.5	18.6	-0.9	29	71	14	16.9	18.6	1.7
Tax revenue	16.8	16.2	-0.6	21	79	14	15.0	16.2	1.2
Taxes on domestic goods and services	6.1	6.1	—	27	73	11	4.7	5.8	1.1
Taxes on income, profits, and capital gains	4.6	5.7	1.1	73	18	10	4.8	4.3	-0.5
Taxes on international trade	7.0	6.0	-1.1	—	100	9	5.4	5.8	0.3
Nontax revenue	2.1	2.2	0.1	79	21	14	2.0	2.4	0.5
Asian countries									
Total revenue	15.1	14.2	-0.9	—	100	4	14.3	14.7	0.4
Tax revenue	13.8	13.1	-0.7	—	100	3	11.6	12.3	0.8
Taxes on domestic goods and services	6.6	5.9	-0.7	50	50	2	5.0	6.1	1.2
Taxes on income, profits, and capital gains	2.5	2.5	—	100	—	1	1.9	2.4	0.5
Taxes on international trade	5.2	4.9	-0.3	—	100	1	4.4	3.4	-0.9
Nontax revenue	2.9	2.7	-0.3	33	67	3	2.8	2.4	-0.4
Western Hemisphere countries									
Total revenue	22.9	23.0	0.1	75	25	4	21.6	24.1	2.5
Tax revenue	15.8	15.9	—	67	33	3	15.9	22.2	6.3
Taxes on domestic goods and services	8.4	8.5	0.1	50	50	2	8.6	10.6	2.0
Taxes on income, profits, and capital gains	5.6	5.8	0.2	100	—	2	5.7	6.7	1.1
Taxes on international trade	3.2	3.3	0.1	100	—	2	4.6	3.9	-0.6
Nontax revenue	3.8	4.0	0.2	67	33	3	5.6	1.9	-3.8
Transition economies									
Total revenue	20.0	19.9	-0.2	67	33	6	17.8	20.5	2.7
Tax revenue	16.9	15.4	-1.4	33	67	6	14.1	16.5	2.3
Taxes on domestic goods and services	5.7	5.4	-0.3	75	25	4	4.7	5.0	0.3
Taxes on income, profits, and capital gains	7.2	7.2	—	50	50	4	5.8	6.0	0.3
Taxes on international trade	3.6	3.2	-0.3	20	80	5	2.8	4.0	1.1
Nontax revenue	3.2	4.3	1.1	83	17	6	3.6	4.0	0.4

Sources: Country authorities; and IMF staff estimates.

[1]Results for the total SAF/ESAF sample are reported in Table 3.

[2]The components do not sum to the total because of differing sample sizes.

[3]Number of countries in the SAF/ESAF sample for which data are available for a given revenue category. If the sample size varies for different columns, the maximum number is given.

[4]Latest year for which data are available.

Table 22. Revenue: Summary of Program Implementation by Initial Revenue Ratio[1]

	Average Program Target[2]	Average Actual During Program	Program Actual Minus Target[2]	Actual ≥ Target	Actual < Target	Number of Countries[3]	Preprogram Year	Latest Year[4]	Latest Year Minus Preprogram Year
	In percent of GDP			Percent of countries			In percent of GDP		
Countries with low initial revenue effort									
Total revenue	10.5	9.3	-1.2	17	83	6	7.3	9.9	2.6
Tax revenue	9.2	8.0	-1.2	20	80	5	6.2	8.7	2.5
Taxes on domestic goods and services	3.9	3.4	-0.4	—	100	1	2.0	3.1	1.1
Taxes on income, profits, and capital gains	1.8	1.9	0.1	100	—	1	1.2	1.3	0.1
Taxes on international trade	5.0	4.7	-0.3	50	50	2	2.9	4.0	1.1
Nontax revenue	1.4	1.2	-0.2	40	60	5	1.1	1.2	0.1
Countries with medium initial revenue effort									
Total revenue	17.6	16.7	-0.9	28	72	18	15.4	16.9	1.5
Tax revenue	14.1	13.2	-0.8	17	83	18	12.2	14.2	2.0
Taxes on domestic goods and services	5.7	5.6	-0.2	27	73	15	4.8	5.0	0.2
Taxes on income, profits, and capital gains	3.2	3.8	0.6	73	27	15	3.5	3.6	0.1
Taxes on international trade	5.2	4.5	-0.8	13	88	16	4.2	5.1	0.9
Nontax revenue	3.0	3.2	0.3	83	17	18	3.2	2.7	-0.5
Countries with high initial revenue effort									
Total revenue	24.6	24.9	0.3	50	50	12	24.6	23.9	-0.6
Tax revenue	20.8	20.7	-0.1	33	58	11	20.8	20.6	-0.2
Taxes on domestic goods and services	5.9	6.2	0.3	57	43	7	6.6	7.7	1.1
Taxes on income, profits, and capital gains	7.8	9.0	1.2	71	29	7	7.2	7.7	0.6
Taxes on international trade	6.5	6.0	-0.5	—	100	7	6.4	5.2	-1.2
Nontax revenue	2.8	3.6	0.8	67	25	11	3.7	3.3	-0.4

Sources: Country authorities; and IMF staff estimates.
[1] Results for the total SAF/ESAF sample are reported in Table 2.
[2] The components do not sum to the total because of differing sample sizes.
[3] Number of countries in the SAF/ESAF sample for which data are available for a given revenue category. If the sample size varies for different columns, the maximum number is given.
[4] Latest year for which data are available.

Table 23. Indicators of Fiscal Adjustment: Total Expenditure and Net Lending
(In percent of GDP)

	(1) Average of Three Years Prior to Program	(2) Pre-program Year	(3) Average from Beginning of Program Until Latest Year (1994 or 1995)	(4) Latest Year (1994 or 1995)[1]	(5)=(4)−(1) Latest Year Minus Three-Year Preprogram Average	(6)=(4)−(2) Latest Year Minus Preprogram Year	(7) Average Program Target	(8) Average Actual During Program	(9)=(8)−(7) Average Program Actual Minus Target	(10) Number of Years Actual Exceeded Program Target	(11) Number of Years Actual Less Than Program Target
Albania	57.0	46.5	42.0	39.9	−17.1	−6.6	45.2	42.6	−2.59	—	2
Bangladesh	16.3	16.1	16.3	17.6	1.3	1.6	17.0	15.9	−1.12	—	6
Benin	23.4	22.4	19.6	21.4	−2.0	−1.0	21.0	19.3	−1.66	1	3
Bolivia	23.2	22.3	28.6	30.9	7.7	8.6	28.1	28.9	0.79	5	2
Burkina Faso	18.9	19.6	21.7	21.0	2.2	1.4	22.9	21.9	−1.04	3	1
Burundi	26.6	23.4	27.0	26.0	−0.5	2.6	31.5	33.2	1.70	4	3
Cambodia	9.6	11.2	16.6	16.6	7.0	5.4	14.3	16.6	2.30	1	—
Côte d'Ivoire	31.6	30.0	27.1	26.3	−5.3	−3.7	28.6	27.1	−1.48	1	1
Equatorial Guinea	24.0	24.8	23.4	19.6	−4.4	−5.2	21.4	19.2	−2.23	2	1
Gambia, The	31.3	26.2	28.6	25.8	−5.5	−0.4	36.2	37.3	1.06	4	2
Ghana	12.8	14.3	17.2	23.7	10.9	9.3	15.8	15.8	−0.03	2	5
Guinea	...	20.8	21.6	17.5	...	−3.3	19.0	21.0	1.95	5	2
Guyana	77.8	66.0	48.0	39.4	−38.4	−26.7	54.4	51.8	−2.52	—	4
Honduras	22.6	22.1	23.9	21.3	−1.3	−0.7	22.4	24.3	1.91	2	1
Kenya	31.7	31.9	34.5	35.1	3.5	3.3	29.4	31.8	2.47	3	3
Kyrgyz Republic	31.9	36.7	28.3	28.1	−3.8	−8.6	39.7	28.3	−11.40	1	1
Lao People's Dem. Rep.	25.1	32.8	21.7	21.0	−4.1	−11.8	29.3	23.8	−5.41	2	4
Lesotho	31.3	33.6	31.5	30.7	−0.6	−3.0	30.7	31.5	0.83	4	3
Madagascar	18.4	16.2	18.6	17.8	−0.6	1.6	24.6	22.8	−1.76	4	4
Malawi	34.1	33.0	32.6	37.6	3.5	4.6	27.5	28.9	1.38	5	2
Mali	28.7	25.7	25.7	24.9	−3.9	−0.8	25.9	25.3	−0.59	1	6
Mauritania	43.3	38.5	31.1	24.8	−18.5	−13.7	31.4	31.1	−0.33	3	4
Mongolia	53.4	38.9	48.5	44.9	−8.4	6.0	43.3	48.5	5.19	3	—
Mozambique	33.0	30.9	45.1	39.1	6.2	8.2	51.8	46.0	−5.82	2	6
Nepal	17.5	18.0	18.0	17.7	0.2	−0.3	18.9	18.4	−0.54	3	3
Nicaragua	27.5	27.5	30.8	31.4	3.8	3.8	29.7	30.3	0.60	1	—
Niger	20.2	21.4	18.6	15.3	−4.9	−6.1	19.9	20.9	1.02	3	1
Pakistan	26.6	26.9	25.2	22.9	−3.7	−4.0	24.9	25.1	0.17	3	2
Senegal	23.7	21.4	20.0	18.3	−5.3	−3.1	19.4	20.2	0.80	7	1
Sierra Leone	17.8	19.1	19.4	19.8	2.0	0.7	19.1	21.0	1.92	3	1
Sri Lanka	33.1	32.5	30.9	30.7	−2.4	−1.7	30.1	30.9	0.82	4	4
Tanzania	27.8	29.4	24.8	22.2	−5.6	−7.3	31.5	28.3	−3.18	1	5
Togo	35.4	32.8	26.6	25.6	−9.8	−7.1	28.4	28.0	−0.47	1	3
Uganda	12.1	9.4	15.9	18.6	6.5	9.2	16.5	16.5	−0.02	4	4

										2	3
Vietnam	22.8	28.5	26.0	24.9	2.1	-3.6	28.5	26.0	-2.49	—	2
Zimbabwe	42.9	44.3	40.6	40.8	-2.1	-3.5	37.5	40.3	2.82	3	—
Average	29.0	27.6	27.1	26.1	-2.6	-1.6	28.2	27.7	-0.5	2.4	2.6
Africa	27.1	25.9	26.0	25.1	-1.6	-0.8	26.8	26.7	-0.1	2.8	2.8
CFA franc countries	25.7	24.8	22.8	21.6	-4.2	-3.2	23.4	22.7	-0.7	2.4	2.1
Other Africa	27.9	26.5	27.7	27.1	-0.1	0.6	28.7	29.0	0.2	3.1	3.1
Other countries	31.7	30.4	28.9	27.7	-4.1	-2.8	30.4	29.4	-1.0	1.8	2.2
Countries without program interruption	28.4	27.8	27.0	26.4	-2.1	-1.4	30.0	28.2	-1.7	1.9	1.9
Countries with one program interruption	33.3	30.2	29.8	28.6	-4.8	-1.7	29.9	30.3	0.4	2.2	2.6
Countries with two program interruptions	27.9	27.9	26.5	25.7	-2.2	-2.2	27.8	27.0	-0.7	2.3	3.2
Countries with three program interruptions	23.6	22.7	24.0	22.4	-0.1	-0.2	24.0	24.3	0.3	3.7	2.2
Transition economies	33.3	32.5	30.5	29.2	-4.1	-3.2	33.4	31.0	-2.4	1.2	1.5

Sources: Country authorities; and IMF staff estimates.
[1]Latest year for which data are available.

Table 24. Indicators of Fiscal Adjustment: Current Expenditure
(In percent of GDP)

	(1) Average of Three Years Prior to Program	(2) Preprogram Year	(3) Average from Beginning of Program Until Latest Year (1994 or 1995)	(4) Latest Year (1994 or 1995)[1]	(5)=(4)−(1) Latest Year Minus Three-Year Preprogram Average	(6)=(4)−(2) Latest Year Minus Preprogram Year	(7) Average Program Target	(8) Average Actual During Program	(9)=(8)−(7) Average Program Actual Minus Target	(10) Number of Years Actual Exceeded Program Target	(11) Number of Years Actual Less Than Program Target
Albania	47.2	42.3	32.1	30.4	−16.8	−11.8	35.9	32.5	−3.4	—	2
Bangladesh	6.8	7.3	8.1	8.2	1.4	0.9	8.3	8.0	−0.3	2	4
Benin	16.5	15.5	13.6	13.6	−2.9	−1.9	13.5	13.2	−0.3	2	2
Bolivia	19.1	17.6	19.4	21.3	2.3	3.8	20.0	19.9	−0.1	4	3
Burkina Faso	12.1	14.1	12.5	11.3	−0.8	−2.8	12.2	12.7	0.5	3	1
Burundi	11.6	10.7	15.2	17.1	5.5	6.4	15.6	17.8	2.2	6	1
Cambodia	7.9	6.9	11.1	11.1	3.2	4.2	9.6	11.2	1.5	1	—
Côte d'Ivoire	28.6	26.9	21.9	20.7	−7.8	−6.2	23.4	21.9	−1.5	1	1
Equatorial Guinea	19.0	20.9	21.2	18.4	−0.6	−2.5	13.1	14.0	0.9	2	1
Gambia, The	19.9	17.4	19.2	17.8	−2.0	0.4	23.5	24.5	1.0	3	3
Ghana	10.6	11.9	12.8	16.8	6.2	4.9	12.0	11.6	−0.4	1	6
Guinea	...	13.0	11.5	9.0	...	−4.0	9.6	11.2	1.7	5	2
Guyana	64.7	55.4	34.7	25.3	−39.4	−30.1	42.3	40.6	−1.7	1	3
Honduras	17.8	17.1	16.7	14.8	−3.0	−2.2	17.2	17.1	−0.1	2	2
Kenya	25.0	26.4	28.0	27.2	2.2	0.8	22.7	24.9	2.1	4	2
Kyrgyz Republic	25.3	27.9	23.4	23.9	−1.4	−3.9	34.5	23.4	−11.0	—	2
Lao People's Dem. Rep.	11.9	12.3	10.9	10.2	−1.7	−2.0	12.8	11.8	−1.0	3	3
Lesotho	20.5	19.5	19.7	21.3	0.7	1.8	19.7	19.7	—	3	4
Madagascar	12.0	10.8	11.0	11.2	−0.8	0.4	12.6	12.9	0.3	3	—
Malawi	25.8	25.0	24.8	27.5	1.7	2.5	20.8	22.1	1.3	5	2
Mali	12.9	12.0	11.9	10.9	−2.0	−1.1	12.1	11.9	−0.2	2	5
Mauritania	27.3	26.9	21.0	18.0	−9.4	−8.9	20.6	20.1	−0.5	4	3
Mongolia	44.0	28.3	28.2	27.6	−16.4	−0.7	22.6	28.2	5.6	3	—
Mozambique	24.5	25.3	22.5	16.6	−7.8	−8.7	26.7	23.2	−3.5	1	7
Nepal	5.9	5.8	6.1	7.4	1.6	1.6	6.5	6.3	−0.1	1	5
Nicaragua	22.1	20.7	20.5	19.7	−2.4	−1.0	20.9	21.3	0.4	1	—
Niger	11.0	11.7	12.0	10.9	−0.1	−0.8	10.6	12.0	1.4	4	—
Pakistan	19.8	20.1	19.4	18.5	−1.3	−1.6	19.0	19.3	0.3	3	2
Senegal	19.8	17.7	15.6	13.0	−6.8	−4.7	15.2	15.7	0.6	6	2
Sierra Leone	14.7	16.3	15.7	16.4	1.7	0.2	14.3	16.9	2.6	4	—
Sri Lanka	19.7	20.1	21.9	23.3	3.6	3.2	20.6	21.7	1.1	5	3
Tanzania	21.7	22.0	19.9	17.6	−4.1	−4.4	22.9	23.1	0.2	1	5
Togo	23.0	23.1	21.6	23.3	0.2	0.2	22.2	21.9	−0.3	1	3
Uganda	9.2	5.9	8.4	8.9	−0.3	3.0	8.6	8.9	0.2	5	3

Vietnam	17.6	21.5	20.3	19.0	1.4	-2.5	21.0	20.3	-0.6	1	—
Zimbabwe	34.6	34.7	33.8	33.9	-0.7	-0.8	31.3	33.8	2.5	3	—
Average	20.9	19.7	18.5	17.8	-2.8	-1.9	18.7	18.8	—	2.6	2.3
Africa	19.1	18.5	17.9	17.3	-1.3	-1.2	17.4	17.9	0.5	3.1	2.5
CFA franc countries	17.9	17.7	16.3	15.3	-2.6	-2.5	15.3	15.4	0.1	2.6	1.9
Other Africa	19.8	19.0	18.8	18.5	-0.5	-0.5	18.6	19.3	0.7	3.4	2.8
Other countries	23.6	21.7	19.5	18.6	-4.9	-3.0	20.8	20.1	-0.7	1.9	2.1
Countries without program interruption	22.0	21.0	19.5	19.2	-2.9	-1.9	22.0	20.3	-1.7	1.8	2.0
Countries with one program interruption	26.0	23.1	20.7	19.2	-6.8	-3.9	20.5	21.4	0.9	2.7	2.1
Countries with two program interruptions	18.3	18.7	17.5	17.1	-1.1	-1.5	17.4	17.6	0.2	2.8	2.8
Countries with three program interruptions	15.1	14.7	15.5	15.3	1.5	0.6	14.0	14.8	0.8	3.5	2.3
Transition economies	25.7	23.2	21.0	20.4	-5.3	-2.8	22.7	21.3	-1.5	1.3	1.3

Sources: Country authorities; and IMF staff estimates.

[1] Latest year for which data are available.

Table 25. Indicators of Fiscal Adjustment: Capital Expenditure and Net Lending
(In percent of GDP)

	(1) Average of Three Years Prior to Program	(2) Preprogram Year	(3) Average from Beginning of Program Until Latest Year (1994 or 1995)[1]	(4) Latest Year (1994 or 1995)[1]	(5)=(4)−(1) Latest Year Minus Three-Year Preprogram Average	(6)=(4)−(2) Latest Year Minus Preprogram Year	(7) Average Program Target	(8) Average Actual During Program	(9)=(8)−(7) Average Program Actual Minus Target	(10) Number of Years Actual Exceeded Program Target	(11) Number of Years Actual Less Than Program Target
Albania	9.7	4.2	9.9	9.4	−0.3	5.2	9.2	9.9	0.7	—	—
Bangladesh	8.7	8.5	7.6	8.9	0.2	0.5	8.2	7.3	−0.9	—	5
Benin	6.9	7.0	6.0	7.8	1.0	0.9	7.0	6.1	−1.0	—	3
Bolivia	4.2	4.8	9.2	9.6	5.4	4.8	8.1	9.0	0.9	6	1
Burkina Faso	6.7	5.5	9.2	9.7	3.0	4.3	10.7	9.2	−1.5	2	2
Burundi	15.0	12.7	11.8	9.0	−6.0	−3.7	15.8	15.4	−0.5	—	6
Cambodia	1.7	4.3	5.5	5.5	3.8	1.1	4.7	5.5	0.8	—	—
Côte d'Ivoire	3.0	3.1	5.1	5.6	2.5	2.5	5.2	5.1	—	—	—
Equatorial Guinea	5.0	3.8	2.3	1.2	−3.8	−2.6	8.3	3.5	−4.8	—	2
Gambia, The	11.4	8.7	9.3	7.3	−4.0	−1.4	12.7	12.7	—	2	4
Ghana	2.2	2.4	3.6	6.2	4.0	3.8	3.2	3.7	0.4	4	3
Guinea	...	7.8	10.0	8.5	...	0.7	9.4	9.7	0.3	3	4
Guyana	13.1	10.6	13.3	14.0	1.0	3.4	12.6	11.3	−1.3	1	3
Honduras	4.8	5.0	7.2	6.5	1.7	1.5	5.2	7.2	2.0	2	—
Kenya	6.5	6.2	7.0	7.9	1.4	1.7	6.6	6.9	0.3	3	3
Kyrgyz Republic	6.6	8.8	4.9	4.1	−2.5	−4.7	5.3	4.9	−0.4	—	1
Lao People's Dem. Rep.	13.2	20.6	10.7	10.8	−2.4	−9.7	16.5	12.0	−4.4	2	4
Lesotho	10.8	14.1	11.8	9.4	−1.4	−4.7	11.0	11.8	0.8	3	4
Madagascar	6.4	5.4	7.6	6.6	0.2	1.2	12.0	9.9	−2.0	—	6
Malawi	8.3	8.0	6.8	7.8	−0.5	−0.2	6.8	6.2	−0.6	2	5
Mali	12.5	10.1	11.3	12.8	0.3	2.6	11.9	11.1	−0.8	—	7
Mauritania	15.5	10.4	9.9	6.8	−8.7	−3.5	10.4	10.1	−0.3	6	—
Mongolia	9.4	10.6	20.2	17.3	7.9	6.8	20.7	20.2	−0.4	1	2
Mozambique	8.5	5.6	22.6	22.5	14.0	16.9	25.1	22.7	−2.3	2	6
Nepal	11.7	12.2	12.0	10.3	−1.3	−1.9	12.5	12.1	−0.4	3	3
Nicaragua	5.4	6.8	10.3	11.7	6.2	4.9	8.8	9.0	0.2	1	—
Niger	8.9	9.4	6.1	4.1	−4.8	−5.3	8.8	8.3	−0.5	—	3
Pakistan	6.7	6.8	5.9	4.4	−2.3	−2.4	5.9	5.8	−0.1	2	3
Senegal	3.4	2.7	3.5	4.8	1.5	2.1	3.4	3.5	0.1	3	5
Sierra Leone	3.1	2.8	3.7	3.4	0.3	0.5	4.8	4.1	−0.7	2	2
Sri Lanka	13.4	12.4	9.0	7.5	−6.0	−4.9	9.6	9.3	−0.3	3	5
Tanzania	5.8	7.4	4.9	4.5	−1.3	−2.9	8.4	5.2	−3.3	1	5
Togo	12.3	9.7	5.0	2.3	−10.0	−7.4	6.3	6.1	−0.2	—	4
Uganda	2.9	3.5	7.4	9.7	6.8	6.2	7.9	7.6	−0.3	4	4

Vietnam	5.2	7.0	5.7	6.0	0.7	-1.1	7.5	5.7	-1.9	—	2
Zimbabwe	8.3	9.6	6.8	7.0	-1.3	-2.6	6.1	6.5	0.3	2	1
Average	7.9	7.7	8.4	8.1	0.2	0.3	9.3	8.7	-0.6	1.9	3.1
Africa	7.8	7.1	7.8	7.5	-0.3	0.4	9.2	8.4	-0.8	2.0	3.6
CFA franc countries	7.3	6.4	6.1	6.0	-1.3	-0.4	7.7	6.6	-1.1	1.1	3.4
Other Africa	8.1	7.5	8.8	8.3	0.3	0.9	10.0	9.5	-0.6	2.5	3.7
Other countries	8.1	8.8	9.4	9.0	0.9	0.2	9.6	9.2	-0.4	1.8	2.2
Countries without program interruption	6.4	6.7	7.5	7.1	0.7	0.4	7.9	7.9	—	1.6	2.1
Countries with one program interruption	7.2	7.1	8.8	9.0	1.8	1.9	9.3	8.7	-0.6	1.5	3.3
Countries with two program interruptions	9.3	8.8	8.7	8.4	-0.9	-0.4	10.0	9.1	-0.9	2.1	3.4
Countries with three program interruptions	8.5	8.0	8.5	7.2	-1.6	-0.9	10.0	9.2	-0.8	2.7	3.2
Transition economies	7.6	9.3	9.5	8.9	1.2	-0.4	10.6	9.7	-0.9	1.0	1.7

Sources: Country authorities; and IMF staff estimates.

[1]Latest year for which data are available.

Table 26. Indicators of Fiscal Adjustment: Wages and Salaries
(In percent of GDP)

	(1) Average of Three Years Prior to Program	(2) Pre-program Year	(3) Average from Beginning of Program Until Latest Year (1994 or 1995)¹	(4) Latest Year (1994 or 1995)¹	(5)=(4)−(1) Latest Year Minus Three-Year Preprogram Average	(6)=(4)−(2) Latest Year Minus Preprogram Year	(7) Average Program Target	(8) Average Actual During Program	(9)=(8)−(7) Average Program Actual Minus Target	(10) Number of Years Actual Exceeded Program Target	(11) Number of Years Actual Less Than Program Target
Albania	10.1	10.6	8.9	9.0	−1.0	−1.6	8.5	8.9	0.4	2	—
Bangladesh	2.5	2.8	2.9	3.1	0.6	0.4	...	...	...	...	...
Benin	10.4	10.1	7.9	6.3	−4.1	−3.8	5.7	6.0	0.2	3	1
Bolivia	7.0	6.4	8.7	10.1	3.0	3.7	10.4	10.8	0.4	4	3
Burkina Faso	7.4	7.6	6.2	5.3	−2.1	−2.3	6.0	6.1	0.1	3	1
Burundi	5.4	5.1	6.6	7.2	1.7	2.1	7.2	7.7	0.6	5	2
Cambodia	...	...	...	...	...	...	4.4	4.7	0.3	1	—
Côte d'Ivoire	11.1	10.7	7.4	6.9	−4.2	−3.8	7.7	7.4	−0.3	1	1
Equatorial Guinea	4.9	5.1	5.4	4.0	−0.9	−1.1	3.5	3.9	0.3	3	—
Gambia, The	7.4	5.8	5.2	6.0	−1.4	0.2	6.1	6.1	0.1	3	3
Ghana	3.8	5.1	5.0	5.7	1.9	0.6	4.9	4.8	−0.1	1	6
Guinea	...	2.8	4.2	4.2	...	1.4	3.7	4.1	0.5	4	3
Guyana	12.6	7.3	6.5	6.3	−6.3	−1.0	8.2	7.5	−0.7	—	4
Honduras	8.3	7.2	7.1	6.7	−1.6	−0.5	7.2	7.1	—	2	1
Kenya	10.4	10.7	9.5	11.1	0.7	0.4	8.2	9.9	1.7	2	—
Kyrgyz Republic	5.7	4.9	6.9	7.1	1.5	2.2	7.4	6.9	−0.6	—	2
Lao People's Dem. Rep.	4.1	4.9	4.9	4.9	0.7	—	5.3	5.5	0.1	3	3
Lesotho	8.7	7.5	8.6	9.7	1.0	2.2	8.7	8.6	−0.1	3	4
Madagascar	6.1	5.3	4.3	3.2	−2.8	−2.0	6.1	5.9	−0.2	—	4
Malawi	5.9	6.3	6.1	8.1	2.2	1.8	5.3	5.5	0.2	5	2
Mali	7.2	6.7	5.4	3.9	−3.3	−2.8	5.4	5.3	−0.1	2	5
Mauritania	11.4	10.4	6.5	5.0	−6.4	−5.4	6.2	6.2	—	3	3
Mongolia	8.2	6.2	5.8	6.5	−1.7	0.3	4.7	5.8	1.1	3	—
Mozambique	5.5	4.8	4.3	4.2	−1.3	−0.6	4.6	4.3	−0.4	4	4
Nepal	2.0	2.0	2.0	2.2	0.2	0.2	2.1	2.0	−0.1	1	1
Nicaragua	9.5	7.4	6.7	6.6	−2.9	−0.8	...	...	...	...	...
Niger	3.9	4.0	5.4	5.3	1.4	1.3	4.2	4.8	0.5	4	—
Pakistan	...	...	...	...	...	...	...	...	...	...	...
Senegal	9.8	9.0	8.1	6.5	−3.4	−2.5	7.7	8.0	0.3	7	1
Sierra Leone	4.5	3.0	3.3	3.6	−0.9	0.6	3.6	3.8	0.2	2	2
Sri Lanka	4.3	4.1	5.1	5.3	1.0	1.2	4.8	5.0	0.1	5	2
Tanzania	6.3	5.6	5.2	5.8	−0.5	0.2	5.8	5.7	−0.1	2	2
Togo	8.4	9.1	9.0	9.2	0.8	0.1	8.7	8.7	—	2	2
Uganda	1.7	1.0	1.7	1.9	0.2	0.9	1.8	1.8	—	4	3

											[1]	[2]
Vietnam	...	...	...	...	...	...	...	...	...	...	...	...
Zimbabwe	14.1	13.5	11.9	11.8	-2.3	-1.7	11.8	11.9	0.1	2.7	2.1
Average	7.1	6.5	6.1	6.1	-0.9	-0.3	6.1	6.3	0.1	2.7	2.1
Africa	7.4	6.8	6.2	6.1	-1.1	-0.6	6.0	6.2	0.2	2.9	2.3
CFA franc countries	7.9	7.8	6.8	5.9	-2.0	-1.8	6.1	6.3	0.1	3.1	1.4
Other Africa	7.0	6.2	5.9	6.3	-0.6	—	6.0	6.2	0.2	2.8	2.9
Other countries	6.8	5.8	5.9	6.2	-0.6	0.4	6.3	6.4	0.1	2.1	1.6
Countries without program interruption	7.4	6.8	6.4	6.8	-0.7	—	6.4	6.3	—	2.0	1.9
Countries with one program interruption	8.0	6.8	6.2	6.4	-1.6	-0.4	6.6	6.9	0.3	2.6	1.8
Countries with two program interruptions	7.1	6.9	6.2	5.9	-1.2	-1.1	6.0	6.0	0.1	2.8	2.6
Countries with three program interruptions	4.8	4.3	5.4	5.5	1.0	1.3	5.4	5.7	0.3	3.4	1.8
Transition economies	7.0	6.7	6.6	6.9	-0.1	0.2	6.1	6.3	0.3	1.8	1.0

Sources: Country authorities; and IMF staff estimates.

[1]Latest year for which data are available.

Table 27. Indicators of Fiscal Adjustment: Subsidies and Transfers
(In percent of GDP)

	(1) Average of Three Years Prior to Program	(2) Pre-program Year	(3) Average from Beginning of Program Until Latest Year (1994 or 1995)	(4) Latest Year (1994 or 1995)[1]	(5)=(4)−(1) Latest Year Minus Three-Year Preprogram Average	(6)=(4)−(2) Latest Year Minus Preprogram Year	(7) Average Program Target	(8) Average Actual During Program	(9)=(8)−(7) Average Program Actual Minus Target	(10) Number of Years Actual Exceeded Program Target	(11) Number of Years Actual Less Than Program Target
Albania	25.1	18.6	14.2	12.7	-12.4	-5.9	17.0	14.2	-2.8	—	2
Bangladesh	1.5	1.6	2.0	2.0	0.5	0.4	...	...	...	...	...
Benin	...	1.1	...	...	...	...	...	...	...	...	...
Bolivia	1.0	...	2.3	3.3	2.3	2.2	2.2	3.0	0.7	3	—
Burkina Faso	1.6	1.6	2.8	2.5	0.9	0.9	...	...	...	...	...
Burundi	1.2	1.3	2.2	2.5	1.3	1.2	2.1	2.5	0.4	5	2
Cambodia	...	...	...	...	...	...	...	...	...	...	...
Côte d'Ivoire	1.6	2.2	2.3	2.3	0.8	0.1	1.0	1.0	0.1	1	—
Equatorial Guinea	...	2.0	2.0	1.0	...	...	0.5	0.8	0.3	1	—
Gambia, The	1.9	2.5	4.2	1.5	-0.4	-0.9	4.5	5.5	1.0	5	—
Ghana	1.8	2.1	2.7	4.3	2.5	2.2	2.6	2.5	-0.1	2	3
Guinea	...	1.5	1.4	1.4	...	—	1.2	1.5	0.2	4	—
Guyana	7.0	7.3	5.7	2.6	-4.5	-4.8	4.6	4.6	—	3	—
Honduras	2.1	2.2	2.6	2.1	—	-0.1	1.9	2.2	0.3	2	—
Kenya	2.8	2.9	3.3	1.3	-1.5	-1.6	...	...	...	...	...
Kyrgyz Republic	12.3	15.9	7.4	5.9	-6.4	-10.0	10.6	7.4	-3.2	—	2
Lao People's Dem. Rep.	—	0.1	1.2	1.5	1.5	1.4	1.4	1.2	-0.2	3	1
Lesotho	...	...	1.6	...	...	...	1.1	...	...	...	...
Madagascar	1.3	1.3	1.3	1.1	-0.1	-0.2	1.6	1.7	0.1	3	—
Malawi	2.3	2.1	2.6	...	...	...	...	...	...	...	...
Mali	0.6	0.5	0.8	1.1	0.5	0.6	0.8	0.9	—	4	2
Mauritania	3.1	2.8	2.2	1.7	-1.4	-1.1	2.0	2.0	—	4	2
Mongolia	21.3	10.0	8.1	6.9	-14.4	-3.1	6.3	7.2	0.9	1	2
Mozambique	7.1	8.8	1.9	1.5	-5.5	-7.3	2.8	2.1	-0.7	1	6
Nepal	...	...	...	...	...	...	...	...	...	...	...
Nicaragua	3.8	4.0	4.8	5.0	1.2	1.0	...	...	...	...	...
Niger	1.7	1.4	1.3	0.6	-1.0	-0.8	1.3	1.3	—	2	2
Pakistan	1.9	2.0	1.2	0.7	-1.2	-1.2	...	...	...	...	...
Senegal	2.6	2.1	1.9	1.8	-0.8	-0.2	1.6	2.0	0.4	3	—
Sierra Leone	3.3	5.0	1.5	2.0	-1.4	-3.0	1.5	2.0	0.5	2	2
Sri Lanka	5.6	5.6	6.1	6.1	0.6	0.6	...	...	...	...	...
Tanzania	2.8	2.9	7.5	7.7	4.8	4.8	...	...	...	...	...
Togo	1.0	1.0	1.4	2.3	1.3	1.3	2.0	1.7	-0.3	1	3
Uganda	...	...	—	...	...	...	0.3	0.3	—	2	1

Vietnam	...	...	...	...	...	...	...	...	...	...	...
Zimbabwe	...	...	...	...	...	...	5.9	6.7	0.8	2	1
Average	4.4	3.9	3.2	3.1	-1.3	-0.9	3.2	3.2	-0.1	2.3	1.9
Africa	2.3	2.5	2.2	2.2	—	-0.3	1.9	2.2	0.2	2.6	2.0
CFA franc countries	1.5	1.5	1.8	1.7	0.3	0.3	1.3	1.5	0.2	2.1	1.4
Other Africa	2.8	3.0	2.5	2.5	-0.2	-0.6	2.3	2.7	0.2	3.0	2.4
Other countries	7.4	6.2	5.1	4.4	-3.0	-1.8	7.0	6.1	-0.8	1.5	1.5
Countries without program interruption	10.2	9.8	4.9	5.6	-4.6	-4.2	5.8	5.7	-1.0	1.6	1.4
Countries with one program interruption	4.8	3.7	4.0	3.4	-1.6	-0.4	3.2	3.5	0.4	2.4	1.2
Countries with two program interruptions	2.6	2.9	2.2	2.4	-0.2	-0.5	2.2	2.3	0.1	2.4	2.4
Countries with three program interruptions	1.4	1.4	1.8	1.8	0.8	0.5	1.3	1.6	0.3	3.3	2.0
Transition economies	14.7	11.1	7.7	6.7	-7.9	-4.4	8.8	7.5	-1.3	1.0	1.8

Sources: Country authorities; and IMF staff estimates.

[1] Latest year for which data are available.

Table 28. Expenditure on General Public Services
(In percent of GDP)

	(1) Average of Three Years Prior to Program	(2) Preprogram Year	(3) Average from Beginning of Program Until Latest Year (1994 or 1995)	(4) Latest Year (1994 or 1995)[1]	(5)=(4)−(1) Latest Year Minus Three-Year Preprogram Average	(6)=(4)−(2) Latest Year Minus Preprogram Year
Albania	...	...	...	...	...	...
Bangladesh	...	...	...	...	...	...
Benin	...	...	...	...	...	...
Bolivia	...	...	...	...	...	...
Burkina Faso	1.5	1.6	2.8	2.8	1.3	1.2
Burundi	...	...	...	...	...	...
Cambodia	...	...	...	...	...	...
Côte d'Ivoire	...	...	...	...	...	...
Equatorial Guinea	...	...	...	...	...	...
Gambia, The	...	...	...	...	...	...
Ghana	2.5	2.6	2.4	2.9	0.5	0.3
Guinea	...	...	...	...	...	...
Guyana	...	...	...	...	...	...
Honduras	...	...	...	...	...	...
Kenya	...	5.8	5.4	4.7	...	−1.1
Kyrgyz Republic	...	2.9	2.1	2.1	...	−0.8
Lao People's Dem. Rep.	...	...	...	...	...	...
Lesotho	3.7	3.0	3.0	3.4	−0.3	0.4
Madagascar	5.1	4.4	4.0	2.8	−2.3	−1.6
Malawi	3.5	4.2	5.0	8.0	4.5	3.8
Mali	...	4.6	2.3	4.1	...	−0.5
Mauritania	...	...	...	...	...	...
Mongolia	2.3	1.8	2.3	2.6	0.3	0.9
Mozambique	...	...	...	...	...	...
Nepal	1.9	1.8	1.0	0.6	−1.3	−1.1
Nicaragua	3.1	3.2	3.1	3.1	—	−0.2
Niger	1.8	2.0	2.4	1.4	−0.3	−0.6
Pakistan	...	...	...	...	...	...
Senegal	6.4	5.6	4.5	3.3	−3.0	−2.3
Sierra Leone	...	...	1.8	2.4	...	...
Sri Lanka	2.2	1.9	2.3	1.6	−0.6	−0.3
Tanzania	8.6	8.5	7.5	6.4	−2.1	−2.1
Togo	4.0	3.7	1.5	2.4	−1.6	−1.3
Uganda	...	...	2.1	3.5	...	...
Vietnam	2.1	2.4	2.4	2.0	−0.1	−0.4
Zimbabwe	...	...	...	...	...	...
Average	3.5	3.5	3.0	3.2	−0.4	−0.3
Africa	4.1	4.2	3.4	3.7	−0.4	−0.3
CFA franc countries	3.4	3.5	2.7	2.8	−0.9	−0.7
Other Africa	4.7	4.8	3.9	4.3	—	—
Other countries	2.3	2.3	2.2	2.0	−0.3	−0.3
Transition economies	2.2	2.3	2.3	2.2	0.1	−0.1

Sources: IMF, *Government Finance Statistics Yearbook* (1995) and staff estimates; and country authorities.
[1] Latest year for which data are available.

Table 29. Expenditure on Economic Services
(In percent of GDP)

	(1) Average of Three Years Prior to Program	(2) Preprogram Year	(3) Average from Beginning of Program Until Latest Year (1994 or 1995)	(4) Latest Year (1994 or 1995)[1]	(5)=(4)–(1) Latest Year Minus Three-Year Preprogram Average	(6)=(4)–(2) Latest Year Minus Preprogram Year
Albania	...	...	...	...	...	...
Bangladesh	...	...	...	...	...	...
Benin	...	...	...	...	...	...
Bolivia	...	...	...	...	...	...
Burkina Faso	2.0	1.7	1.8	2.2	0.2	0.5
Burundi	...	...	...	...	...	...
Cambodia	...	...	...	...	...	...
Côte d'Ivoire	3.0	...	...	...	...	...
Equatorial Guinea	...	...	...	...	...	...
Gambia, The	...	...	...	...	...	...
Ghana	2.4	2.2	2.4	2.2	–0.2	0.1
Guinea	...	...	...	...	...	...
Guyana	...	...	...	...	...	...
Honduras	...	...	...	...	...	...
Kenya	...	8.9	8.1	8.4	...	–0.5
Kyrgyz Republic	...	5.7	1.9	2.0	...	–3.7
Lao People's Dem. Rep.	...	...	...	...	...	...
Lesotho	12.0	12.5	11.5	11.7	–0.3	–0.9
Madagascar	5.7	4.8	6.3	5.3	–0.4	0.5
Malawi	4.0	3.8	4.8	10.9	7.0	7.1
Mali	...	11.7	9.5	11.9	...	0.2
Mauritania	...	...	...	...	...	...
Mongolia	11.0	2.5	8.1	7.6	–3.4	5.2
Mozambique	...	...	...	...	...	...
Nepal	9.1	9.1	8.3	6.9	–2.1	–2.2
Nicaragua	4.1	4.3	3.7	3.7	–0.5	–0.7
Niger	1.5	1.3	6.7	3.1	1.6	1.8
Pakistan	0.8	0.7	0.4	0.1	–0.7	–0.6
Senegal	1.2	1.1	0.7	0.3	–0.9	–0.7
Sierra Leone	...	...	1.3	1.4	...	...
Sri Lanka	10.7	9.2	5.8	5.0	–5.7	–4.2
Tanzania	6.2	5.8	5.6	8.0	1.8	2.2
Togo	1.3	1.3	2.5	2.3	1.0	1.1
Uganda	...	...	0.9	0.5	...	...
Vietnam	...	...	...	...	...	...
Zimbabwe	...	...	...	...	...	...
Average	5.0	5.1	4.8	4.9	–0.2	0.3
Africa	3.9	5.0	4.8	5.3	1.1	1.0
CFA franc countries	1.8	3.4	4.2	4.0	0.5	0.6
Other Africa	6.1	6.3	5.1	6.1	1.6	1.4
Other countries	7.1	5.3	4.7	4.2	–2.5	–1.0
Transition economies	11.0	4.1	5.0	4.8	–3.4	0.7

Sources: IMF, *Government Finance Statistics Yearbook* (1995) and staff estimates; and country authorities.

[1] Latest year for which data are available.

Table 30. Military Spending
(In percent of GDP)

	(1) Average of Three Years Prior to Program	(2) Preprogram Year	(3) Average from Beginning of Program Until Latest Year (1994 or 1995)	(4) Latest Year (1994 or 1995)[1]	(5)=(4)−(1) Latest Year Minus Three-Year Preprogram Average	(6)=(4)−(2) Latest Year Minus Preprogram Year
Albania	...	...	...	...	...	...
Bangladesh	1.2	1.2	1.5	1.5	0.3	0.3
Benin	...	...	...	...	...	...
Bolivia	...	2.0	2.1	2.1	...	0.1
Burkina Faso	2.8	3.1	2.3	2.2	−0.6	−0.9
Burundi	...	...	...	...	...	...
Cambodia	4.1	4.1	6.5	6.5	2.4	2.4
Côte d'Ivoire	1.5	...	...	...	...	...
Equatorial Guinea	...	...	...	...	...	...
Gambia, The	...	...	0.7	0.7	...	...
Ghana	0.8	0.9	0.7	0.7	−0.1	−0.2
Guinea	...	...	1.8	1.4	...	...
Guyana	...	...	...	...	...	...
Honduras	...	...	...	...	...	...
Kenya	...	3.3	2.4	1.9	...	−1.4
Kyrgyz Republic	...	0.7	1.1	1.4	...	0.7
Lao People's Dem. Rep.	...	...	...	...	...	...
Lesotho	4.4	4.1	3.6	3.5	−0.9	−0.7
Madagascar	...	...	...	...	...	...
Malawi	2.0	1.8	1.3	1.4	−0.6	−0.4
Mali	2.5	2.3	2.2	2.4	−0.1	0.1
Mauritania	...	6.0	3.8	2.6	...	−3.4
Mongolia	3.4	2.0	2.9	3.1	−0.4	1.1
Mozambique	...	...	7.5	4.0	...	...
Nepal	1.2	1.2	1.0	0.9	−0.3	−0.3
Nicaragua	2.4	2.0	1.9	1.9	−0.5	−0.2
Niger	0.7	0.8	0.8	0.7	−0.1	−0.1
Pakistan	7.0	7.0	6.3	5.6	−1.4	−1.4
Senegal	2.5	2.3	1.9	1.5	−1.0	−0.8
Sierra Leone	...	...	2.3	4.1	...	...
Sri Lanka	2.8	3.1	2.8	4.1	1.4	1.1
Tanzania	4.3	4.5	2.2	1.6	−2.7	−2.9
Togo	3.4	3.6	2.9	3.9	0.5	0.3
Uganda	...	...	2.2	2.1	...	...
Vietnam	...	...	...	...	...	...
Zimbabwe	5.7	5.4	4.1	3.5	−2.2	−1.9
Average	2.9	2.9	2.6	2.5	−0.4	−0.4
Africa	2.8	3.2	2.5	2.2	−0.8	−1.0
CFA franc countries	2.2	2.4	2.0	2.1	−0.3	−0.3
Other Africa	3.4	3.7	2.7	2.3	−1.3	−1.6
Other countries	3.2	2.6	2.9	3.0	0.2	0.4
Transition economies	3.8	2.2	3.5	3.6	1.0	1.4

Sources: IMF, *Government Finance Statistics Yearbook* (1995) and staff estimates; and country authorities.

[1] Latest year for which data are available.

Table 31. Index of Real Education Spending[1]

	(1) Number of Years Covered[2]	(2) Average of Three Years Prior to Program	(3) Preprogram Year	(4) Latest Year Available[3]	(5)=(4)−(2) Latest Year Minus Three-Year Preprogram Average	(6)=(4)−(3) Latest Year Minus Preprogram Year	(7) Annual Rate of Change Between Latest Year and Preprogram Year
Bangladesh[4]	9	97	100	277	180	177	12.0
Bolivia[5]	7	...	100	247	...	147	13.8
Burkina Faso	3	98	100	122	24	22	6.9
Cambodia[4]	2	91	100	173	83	73	31.7
Côte d'Ivoire	2	100	100	68	−33	−32	−17.6
Ghana	9	75	100	224	150	124	9.4
Honduras	4	...	100	117	...	17	3.9
Kenya	8	...	100	153	...	53	5.4
Kyrgyz Republic	2	...	100	116	...	16	7.9
Lesotho	8	88	100	223	135	123	10.6
Madagascar	9	102	100	84	−18	−16	−1.9
Malawi	7	98	100	116	18	16	2.1
Mali	8	...	100	85	...	−15	−1.9
Mongolia	3	165	100	110	−55	10	3.1
Nepal[4]	8	99	100	175	76	75	7.3
Nicaragua	1	101	100	120	19	20	19.8
Niger	9	98	100	138	40	38	3.6
Senegal	9	102	100	106	4	6	0.7
Sri Lanka	8	106	100	168	62	68	6.7
Tanzania	7	95	100	161	66	61	7.0
Togo	6	110	100	141	31	41	5.8
Vietnam	2	66	100	118	52	18	8.8
Zimbabwe	5	125	100	107	−18	7	1.4
All countries[6]							
Average	6	101	100	146	45	46	6.4
Median	7	99	100	122	35	22	6.7
African countries							
Average	7	99	100	133	36	33	2.4
Median	8	98	100	122	24	22	3.6
CFA franc							
countries—average	6	102	100	110	13	10	−0.4
Other Africa—average	8	97	100	153	56	53	4.9
Other countries							
Average	5	104	100	162	60	62	11.5
Median	4	99	100	144	62	44	8.3

Sources: Data for Bangladesh are from Budgetary Summary Statements of the Ministry of Finance of Bangladesh, various years, World Bank (1996a), and IMF staff estimates; for Bolivia, Cambodia, the Kyrgyz Republic, Mongolia, and Vietnam, from IMF, *Recent Economic Developments*, various issues; for Burkina Faso, Ghana, Nepal, and Sri Lanka, from IMF, *Government Finance Statistics* database; for Côte d'Ivoire, Kenya, Lesotho, Madagascar, Malawi, Mali, Niger, Senegal, Togo, and Zimbabwe, from IMF, *Recent Economic Developments*, various issues, and staff estimates; for Honduras and Nicaragua, from IMF staff estimates; and for Tanzania, from the World Bank (1996f).

[1]GDP deflator is used to deflate spending.

[2]Number of years between the preprogram year and the latest year for which data are available.

[3]Latest year is for the period 1993–95.

[4]For Bangladesh, Cambodia, and Nepal, data in column (2) are based on a two-year preprogram average instead of a three-year average.

[5]For Bolivia, data for the preprogram year are not available; instead, data from the first program year are presented in column (3).

[6]Due to data omissions, differences given in columns (5) and (6) for aggregated countries may not equal column differences.

Table 32. Index of Per Capita Real Education Spending[1]

	(1) Number of Years Covered[2]	(2) Average of Three Years Prior to Program	(3) Preprogram Year	(4) Latest Year Available[3]	(5)=(4)–(2) Latest Year Minus Three-Year Preprogram Average	(6)=(4)–(3) Latest Year Minus Preprogram Year	(7) Annual Rate of Change Between Latest Year and Preprogram Year
Bangladesh[4]	9	98	100	234	136	134	9.9
Bolivia[5]	7	...	100	214	...	114	11.5
Burkina Faso	3	101	100	113	12	13	4.1
Cambodia[4]	2	139	100	169	30	69	29.9
Côte d'Ivoire	2	105	100	63	–42	–37	–20.6
Ghana	9	77	100	176	99	76	6.5
Honduras	4	...	100	103	...	3	0.8
Kenya	8	...	100	110	...	10	1.2
Kyrgyz Republic	2	...	100	113	...	13	6.1
Lesotho	8	90	100	184	94	84	7.9
Madagascar	9	103	100	65	–39	–35	–4.7
Malawi	7	101	100	92	–9	–8	–1.1
Mali	8	...	100	83	...	–17	–2.3
Mongolia	3	169	100	104	–65	4	1.3
Nepal[4]	8	102	100	143	41	43	4.6
Nicaragua	1	104	100	116	12	16	16.0
Niger	9	101	100	105	4	5	0.6
Senegal	9	105	100	82	–24	–18	–2.2
Sri Lanka	8	108	100	150	42	50	5.2
Tanzania	7	98	100	129	31	29	3.7
Togo	6	114	100	113	0	13	2.1
Vietnam	2	67	100	113	46	13	6.5
Zimbabwe	5	130	100	98	–32	–2	–0.5
All countries[6]							
Average	6	106	100	125	19	25	3.8
Median	7	103	100	113	12	13	3.7
African countries							
Average	7	102	100	109	9	9	–0.4
Median	8	101	100	105	0	5	0.6
CFA franc							
countries—average	6	105	100	93	–10	–7	–3.1
Other Africa—average	8	100	100	122	24	22	1.9
Other countries							
Average	5	112	100	146	35	46	9.2
Median	4	104	100	130	41	30	6.3

Sources: Data for Bangladesh are from Budgetary Summary Statements of the Ministry of Finance of Bangladesh, various years, World Bank (1996a), and IMF staff estimates; for Bolivia, Cambodia, the Kyrgyz Republic, Mongolia, and Vietnam, from IMF, *Recent Economic Developments,* various issues; for Burkina Faso, Ghana, Nepal, and Sri Lanka, from IMF, *Government Finance Statistics* database; for Côte d'Ivoire, Kenya, Lesotho, Madagascar, Malawi, Mali, Niger, Senegal, Togo, and Zimbabwe, from IMF, *Recent Economic Developments,* various issues, and staff estimates; for Honduras and Nicaragua, from IMF staff estimates; and for Tanzania, from the World Bank (1996f).

[1]GDP deflator is used to deflate spending.

[2]Number of years between the preprogram year and the latest year for which data are available.

[3]Latest year is for the period 1993–95.

[4]For Bangladesh, Cambodia, and Nepal, data in column (2) are based on a two-year preprogram average instead of a three-year average.

[5]For Bolivia, data for the preprogram year are not available; instead, data from the first program year are presented in column (3).

[6]Due to data omissions, differences given in columns (5) and (6) for aggregated countries may not equal column differences.

Table 33. Education Spending in Relation to GDP

	(1) Number of Years Covered[1]	(2) Average of Three Years Prior to Program	(3) Preprogram Year	(4) Latest Year Available[2]	(5)=(4)–(2) Latest Year Minus Three-Year Preprogram Average	(6)=(4)–(3) Latest Year Minus Preprogram Year
Bangladesh[3]	9	1.5	1.5	2.7	1.2	1.2
Bolivia[4]	7	...	2.9	5.5	...	2.6
Burkina Faso	3	2.7	2.7	3.0	0.3	0.3
Cambodia[3]	2	0.6	0.6	1.0	0.4	0.4
Côte d'Ivoire	2	6.8	6.8	4.3	–2.5	–2.5
Ghana	9	2.6	3.3	5.2	2.6	1.9
Honduras	4	...	3.8	3.7	...	–0.1
Kenya	8	...	6.9	8.0	...	1.1
Kyrgyz Republic	2	...	3.9	6.0	...	2.1
Lesotho	8	4.5	4.9	7.9	3.4	3.0
Madagascar	9	2.9	2.6	2.0	–0.9	–0.6
Malawi	7	2.6	2.7	3.1	0.5	0.5
Mali	8	...	4.0	3.4	...	–0.6
Mongolia	3	9.2	6.3	6.6	–2.7	0.3
Nepal[3]	8	2.2	2.2	2.3	0.1	0.1
Nicaragua	1	4.4	4.4	4.9	0.5	0.6
Niger	9	2.5	2.4	2.9	0.4	0.5
Senegal	9	3.9	3.6	3.2	–0.8	–0.5
Sri Lanka	8	2.7	2.5	2.9	0.2	0.4
Tanzania	7	2.0	2.0	2.5	0.5	0.5
Togo	6	3.9	3.5	4.8	0.9	1.3
Vietnam	2	1.5	2.1	2.1	0.6	0.0
Zimbabwe	5	7.5	7.8	8.0	0.5	0.2
All countries[5]						
Average	6	3.6	3.6	4.2	0.3	0.5
Median	7	2.7	3.3	3.4	0.5	0.4
African countries						
Average	7	3.8	4.1	4.5	0.5	0.4
Median	8	2.9	3.5	3.4	0.5	0.5
CFA franc countries—average	6	4.0	3.8	3.6	–0.3	–0.2
Other Africa—average	8	3.7	4.3	5.2	1.1	0.9
Other countries						
Average	5	3.2	3.0	3.8	0.1	0.8
Median	4	2.2	2.7	3.3	0.4	0.4

Sources: Data for Bangladesh are from Budgetary Summary Statements of the Ministry of Finance of Bangladesh, various years, World Bank (1996a), and IMF staff estimates; for Bolivia, Cambodia, the Kyrgyz Republic, Mongolia, and Vietnam, from IMF, *Recent Economic Developments,* various issues; for Burkina Faso, Ghana, Nepal, and Sri Lanka, from IMF, *Government Finance Statistics* database; for Côte d'Ivoire, Kenya, Lesotho, Madagascar, Malawi, Mali, Niger, Senegal, Togo, and Zimbabwe, from IMF, *Recent Economic Developments,* various issues, and staff estimates; for Honduras and Nicaragua, from IMF staff estimates; and for Tanzania, from the World Bank (1996f).

[1]Number of years between the preprogram year and the latest year for which data are available.

[2]Latest year is for the period 1993–95.

[3]For Bangladesh, Cambodia, and Nepal, data in column (2) are based on a two-year preprogram average instead of a three-year average.

[4]For Bolivia, data for the preprogram year are not available; instead, data from the first program year are presented in column (3).

[5]Due to data omissions, differences given in columns (5) and (6) for aggregated countries may not equal column differences.

Table 34. Education Spending in Relation to Total Spending

	(1) Number of Years Covered[1]	(2) Average of Three Years Prior to Program	(3) Preprogram Year	(4) Latest Year Available[2]	(5)=(4)–(2) Latest Year Minus Three-Year Preprogram Average	(6)=(4)–(3) Latest Year Minus Preprogram Year
Bangladesh[3]	9	9.4	9.4	15.6	6.2	6.2
Bolivia[4]	7	...	12.3	18.0	...	5.7
Burkina Faso	3	18.0	18.3	17.9	–0.1	–0.4
Cambodia[3]	2	5.7	5.3	6.0	0.3	0.7
Côte d'Ivoire	2	21.5	22.6	16.4	–5.1	–6.2
Ghana	9	20.8	23.9	22.3	1.5	–1.7
Honduras	4	...	15.6	16.6	...	1.0
Kenya	8	...	21.6	22.7	...	1.1
Kyrgyz Republic	2	...	10.7	21.5	...	10.8
Lesotho	8	14.3	14.6	25.2	10.9	10.6
Madagascar	9	16.0	16.2	11.5	–4.5	–4.7
Malawi	7	7.7	8.2	6.1	–1.6	–2.1
Mali	8	...	15.6	13.7	...	–1.8
Mongolia	3	17.3	16.2	14.6	–2.7	–1.6
Nepal[3]	8	11.8	11.5	13.3	1.5	1.8
Nicaragua	1	15.3	14.6	15.5	0.2	0.9
Niger	9	21.3	20.9	22.2	0.9	1.3
Senegal	9	19.8	20.4	24.3	4.5	3.9
Sri Lanka	8	8.3	7.8	10.1	1.9	2.3
Tanzania	7	6.6	6.4	8.4	1.8	2.0
Togo	6	10.9	10.7	18.8	7.8	8.1
Vietnam	2	6.5	7.5	8.5	2.0	1.0
Zimbabwe	5	17.4	17.6	19.6	2.2	2.0
All countries[5]						
Average	6	13.8	14.3	16.0	1.5	1.8
Median	7	14.8	14.6	16.4	1.5	1.1
African countries						
Average	7	15.8	16.7	17.6	1.7	0.9
Median	8	17.4	17.6	18.8	1.5	1.1
CFA franc countries—average	6	18.3	18.1	18.9	1.6	0.8
Other Africa—average	8	13.8	15.5	16.5	1.7	1.0
Other countries						
Average	5	10.6	11.1	14.0	1.3	2.9
Median	4	9.4	11.1	15.0	1.5	1.4

Sources: Data for Bangladesh are from Budgetary Summary Statements of the Ministry of Finance of Bangladesh, various years, World Bank (1996a), and IMF staff estimates; for Bolivia, Cambodia, the Kyrgyz Republic, Mongolia, and Vietnam, from IMF, *Recent Economic Developments*, various issues; for Burkina Faso, Ghana, Nepal, and Sri Lanka, from IMF, *Government Finance Statistics* database; for Côte d'Ivoire, Kenya, Lesotho, Madagascar, Malawi, Mali, Niger, Senegal, Togo, and Zimbabwe, from IMF, *Recent Economic Developments*, various issues, and staff estimates; for Honduras and Nicaragua, from IMF staff estimates; and for Tanzania, from the World Bank (1996f).

[1]Number of years between the preprogram year and the latest year for which data are available.

[2]Latest year is for the period 1993–95.

[3]For Bangladesh, Cambodia, and Nepal, data in column (2) are based on a two-year preprogram average instead of a three-year average.

[4]For Bolivia, data for the preprogram year are not available; instead, data from the first program year are presented in column (3).

[5]Due to data omissions, differences given in columns (5) and (6) for aggregated countries may not equal column differences

Table 35. Index of Real Health Spending[1]

	(1) Number of Years Covered[2]	(2) Average of Three Years Prior to Program	(3) Preprogram Year	(4) Latest Year Available[3]	(5)=(4)−(2) Latest Year Minus Three-Year Preprogram Average	(6)=(4)−(3) Latest Year Minus Preprogram Year	(7) Annual Rate of Change Between Latest Year and Preprogram Year
Bangladesh[4]	9	107	100	287	180	187	12.4
Bolivia[5]	7	...	100	205	...	105	10.8
Burkina Faso	3	99	100	140	41	40	11.8
Cambodia[4]	2	108	100	274	166	174	65.4
Côte d'Ivoire	2	106	100	79	−26	−21	−10.9
Ghana	9	92	100	201	110	101	8.1
Honduras	4	...	100	117	...	17	4.0
Kenya	8	...	100	162	...	62	6.2
Kyrgyz Republic	2	...	100	105	...	5	2.6
Lesotho	8	78	100	173	94	73	7.1
Madagascar	9	101	100	128	27	28	2.8
Malawi	7	122	100	138	16	38	4.7
Mali	8	...	100	94	...	−6	−0.8
Mongolia	3	148	100	136	−12	36	10.9
Nepal[4]	8	103	100	182	80	82	7.8
Nicaragua	1	100	100	117	17	17	16.6
Niger	9	95	100	229	134	129	9.6
Senegal	9	105	100	117	11	17	1.7
Sri Lanka	8	81	100	139	58	39	4.2
Tanzania	7	94	100	195	102	95	10.0
Togo	6	97	100	143	46	43	6.2
Vietnam	2	79	100	99	20	−1	−0.4
Zimbabwe	5	132	100	117	−15	17	3.2
All countries[6]							
Average	6	103	100	156	58	56	8.4
Median	7	101	100	139	44	39	6.2
African countries							
Average	7	102	100	147	49	47	4.6
Median	8	99	100	140	41	40	6.2
CFA franc							
countries—average	6	100	100	134	41	34	2.9
Other Africa—average	8	103	100	159	56	59	6.0
Other countries							
Average	5	104	100	166	73	66	13.4
Median	4	103	100	138	58	38	9.3

Sources: Data for Bangladesh are from Budgetary Summary Statements of the Ministry of Finance of Bangladesh, various years, World Bank (1996a), and IMF staff estimates; for Bolivia, Cambodia, the Kyrgyz Republic, Mongolia, and Vietnam, from IMF, *Recent Economic Developments,* various issues; for Burkina Faso, Ghana, Nepal, and Sri Lanka, from IMF, *Government Finance Statistics* database; for Côte d'Ivoire, Kenya, Lesotho, Madagascar, Malawi, Mali, Niger, Senegal, Togo, and Zimbabwe, from IMF, *Recent Economic Developments,* various issues, and staff estimates; for Honduras and Nicaragua, from IMF staff estimates; and for Tanzania, from the World Bank (1996f).

[1]GDP deflator is used to deflate spending.

[2]Number of years between the preprogram year and the latest year for which data are available.

[3]Latest year is for the period 1993–95.

[4]For Bangladesh, Cambodia, and Nepal, data in column (2) are based on a two-year preprogram average instead of a three-year average.

[5]For Bolivia, data for the preprogram year are not available; instead, data from the first program year are presented in column (3).

[6]Due to data omissions, differences given in columns (5) and (6) for aggregated countries may not equal column differences.

Table 36. Index of Per Capita Real Health Spending[1]

	(1) Number of Years Covered[2]	(2) Average of Three Years Prior to Program	(3) Preprogram Year	(4) Latest Year Available[3]	(5)=(4)−(2) Latest Year Minus Three-Year Preprogram Average	(6)=(4)−(3) Latest Year Minus Preprogram Year	(7) Annual Rate of Change Between Latest Year and Preprogram Year
Bangladesh[4]	9	108	100	243	134	143	10.4
Bolivia[5]	7	...	100	177	...	77	8.5
Burkina Faso	3	102	100	129	28	29	8.9
Cambodia[4]	2	110	100	266	156	166	63.2
Côte d'Ivoire	2	110	100	74	−36	−26	−14.2
Ghana	9	95	100	158	63	58	5.2
Honduras	4	...	100	104	...	4	0.9
Kenya	8	...	100	117	...	17	2.0
Kyrgyz Republic	2	...	100	102	...	2	0.9
Lesotho	8	80	100	142	62	42	4.5
Madagascar	9	103	100	99	−5	−1	−0.2
Malawi	7	127	100	110	−16	10	1.4
Mali	8	...	100	91	...	−9	−1.2
Mongolia	3	151	100	129	−22	29	8.9
Nepal[4]	8	105	100	149	44	49	5.1
Nicaragua	1	103	100	113	10	13	12.9
Niger	9	98	100	175	77	75	6.4
Senegal	9	108	100	90	−19	−10	−1.2
Sri Lanka	8	82	100	124	42	24	2.8
Tanzania	7	97	100	157	60	57	6.6
Togo	6	100	100	116	15	16	2.5
Vietnam	2	80	100	95	15	−5	−2.5
Zimbabwe	5	137	100	107	−30	7	1.3
All countries[6]							
Average	6	105	100	133	32	33	5.8
Median	7	103	100	117	21	17	2.8
African countries							
Average	7	105	100	120	18	20	1.7
Median	8	102	100	116	15	16	2.0
CFA franc							
countries—average	6	104	100	112	13	12	0.2
Other Africa—average	8	106	100	127	22	27	3.0
Other countries							
Average	5	106	100	150	54	50	11.1
Median	4	105	100	127	42	27	6.8

Sources: Data for Bangladesh are from Budgetary Summary Statements of the Ministry of Finance of Bangladesh, various years, World Bank (1996a), and IMF staff estimates; for Bolivia, Cambodia, the Kyrgyz Republic, Mongolia, and Vietnam, from IMF, *Recent Economic Developments*, various issues; for Burkina Faso, Ghana, Nepal, and Sri Lanka, from IMF, *Government Finance Statistics* database; for Côte d'Ivoire, Kenya, Lesotho, Madagascar, Malawi, Mali, Niger, Senegal, Togo, and Zimbabwe, from IMF, *Recent Economic Developments*, various issues, and staff estimates; for Honduras and Nicaragua, from IMF staff estimates; and for Tanzania, from the World Bank (1996f).

[1]GDP deflator is used to deflate spending.

[2]Number of years between the preprogram year and the latest year for which data are available.

[3]Latest year is for the period 1993–95.

[4]For Bangladesh, Cambodia, and Nepal, data in column (2) are based on a two-year preprogram average instead of a three-year average.

[5]For Bolivia, data for the preprogram year are not available; instead, data from the first program year are presented in column (3).

[6]Due to data omissions, differences given in columns (5) and (6) for aggregated countries may not equal column differences.

Table 37. Health Spending in Relation to GDP

	(1) Number of Years Covered[1]	(2) Average of Three Years Prior to Program	(3) Preprogram Year	(4) Latest Year Available[2]	(5)=(4)-(2) Latest Year Minus Three-Year Preprogram Average	(6)=(4)-(3) Latest Year Minus Preprogram Year
Bangladesh[3]	9	0.7	0.6	1.2	0.5	0.6
Bolivia[4]	7	...	1.3	2.1	...	0.8
Burkina Faso	3	1.0	1.0	1.2	0.3	0.2
Cambodia[3]	2	0.2	0.2	0.5	0.3	0.3
Côte d'Ivoire	2	1.4	1.3	1.0	-0.4	-0.3
Ghana	9	1.1	1.1	1.6	0.5	0.5
Honduras	4	...	2.7	2.7	...	-0.1
Kenya	8	...	2.0	2.5	...	0.5
Kyrgyz Republic	2	...	2.4	3.4	...	0.9
Lesotho	8	2.1	2.5	3.2	1.1	0.6
Madagascar	9	0.9	0.8	0.9	0.0	0.1
Malawi	7	1.9	1.6	2.2	0.3	0.6
Mali	8	...	1.9	1.8	...	-0.1
Mongolia	3	4.9	3.7	4.8	-0.1	1.1
Nepal[3]	8	0.9	0.8	0.9	0.0	0.1
Nicaragua	1	3.9	3.9	4.3	0.4	0.4
Niger	9	0.8	0.8	1.5	0.8	0.8
Senegal	9	0.8	0.7	0.7	-0.1	0.0
Sri Lanka	8	1.4	1.7	1.7	0.2	-0.1
Tanzania	7	1.4	1.4	2.1	0.8	0.7
Togo	6	1.2	1.2	1.7	0.5	0.5
Vietnam	2	1.0	1.2	1.0	0.0	-0.2
Zimbabwe	5	2.5	2.5	2.8	0.3	0.3
All countries[5]						
Average	6	1.6	1.6	2.0	0.3	0.4
Median	7	1.1	1.3	1.7	0.3	0.4
African countries						
Average	7	1.4	1.5	1.8	0.4	0.3
Median	8	1.2	1.3	1.7	0.3	0.5
CFA franc countries—average	6	1.0	1.1	1.3	0.2	0.2
Other Africa—average	8	1.6	1.7	2.2	0.5	0.5
Other countries						
Average	5	1.9	1.9	2.2	0.2	0.4
Median	4	1.0	1.5	1.9	0.2	0.3

Sources: Data for Bangladesh are from Budgetary Summary Statements of the Ministry of Finance of Bangladesh, various years, World Bank (1996a), and IMF staff estimates; for Bolivia, Cambodia, the Kyrgyz Republic, Mongolia, and Vietnam, from IMF, *Recent Economic Developments,* various issues; for Burkina Faso, Ghana, Nepal, and Sri Lanka, from IMF, *Government Finance Statistics* database; for Côte d'Ivoire, Kenya, Lesotho, Madagascar, Malawi, Mali, Niger, Senegal, Togo, and Zimbabwe, from IMF, *Recent Economic Developments,* various issues, and staff estimates; for Honduras and Nicaragua, from IMF staff estimates; and for Tanzania, from the World Bank (1996f).

[1]Number of years between the preprogram year and the latest year for which data are available.

[2]Latest year is for the period 1993–95.

[3]For Bangladesh, Cambodia, and Nepal, data in column (2) are based on a two-year preprogram average instead of a three-year average.

[4]For Bolivia, data for the preprogram year are not available; instead, data from the first program year are presented in column (3).

[5]Due to data omissions, differences given in columns (5) and (6) for aggregated countries may not equal column differences.

Table 38. Health Spending in Relation to Total Spending

	(1) Number of Years Covered[1]	(2) Average of Three Years Prior to Program	(3) Preprogram Year	(4) Latest Year Available[2]	(5)=(4)–(2) Latest Year Minus Three-Year Preprogram Average	(6)=(4)–(3) Latest Year Minus Preprogram Year
Bangladesh[3]	9	4.4	4.0	6.9	2.5	2.9
Bolivia[4]	7	...	5.6	6.8	...	1.2
Burkina Faso	3	6.4	6.5	7.2	0.9	0.8
Cambodia[3]	2	2.1	1.6	3.0	0.8	1.3
Côte d'Ivoire	2	4.4	4.4	3.7	–0.7	–0.7
Ghana	9	8.9	8.3	6.9	–2.0	–1.4
Honduras	4	...	11.3	12.0	...	0.8
Kenya	8	...	6.4	7.1	...	0.7
Kyrgyz Republic	2	...	6.7	12.1	...	5.4
Lesotho	8	6.6	7.6	10.1	3.5	2.5
Madagascar	9	5.0	5.1	5.5	0.5	0.4
Malawi	7	5.6	4.8	4.2	–1.4	–0.5
Mali	8	...	7.5	7.3	...	–0.3
Mongolia	3	9.1	9.5	10.6	1.5	1.1
Nepal[3]	8	4.7	4.4	5.3	0.6	0.9
Nicaragua	1	13.4	13.0	13.4	0.0	0.4
Niger	9	6.4	6.5	11.5	5.1	5.0
Senegal	9	4.0	4.0	5.3	1.3	1.2
Sri Lanka	8	4.4	5.4	5.9	1.5	0.4
Tanzania	7	4.6	4.5	7.2	2.6	2.7
Togo	6	3.3	3.7	6.6	3.3	2.9
Vietnam	2	4.5	4.2	4.0	–0.4	–0.2
Zimbabwe	5	5.8	5.6	6.9	1.0	1.2
All countries[5]						
Average	6	5.8	6.1	7.4	1.1	1.3
Median	7	4.8	5.6	6.9	0.9	0.9
African countries						
Average	7	5.5	5.8	6.9	1.3	1.1
Median	8	5.6	5.6	6.9	1.0	0.8
CFA franc countries—average	6	4.9	5.4	6.9	2.0	1.5
Other Africa—average	8	6.1	6.0	6.8	0.7	0.8
Other countries						
Average	5	6.1	6.6	8.0	0.9	1.4
Median	4	4.5	5.5	6.8	0.8	1.0

Sources: Data for Bangladesh are from Budgetary Summary Statements of the Ministry of Finance of Bangladesh, various years, World Bank (1996a), and IMF staff estimates; for Bolivia, Cambodia, the Kyrgyz Republic, Mongolia, and Vietnam, from IMF, *Recent Economic Developments,* various issues; for Burkina Faso, Ghana, Nepal, and Sri Lanka, from IMF, *Government Finance Statistics* database; for Côte d'Ivoire, Kenya, Lesotho, Madagascar, Malawi, Mali, Niger, Senegal, Togo, and Zimbabwe, from IMF, *Recent Economic Developments,* various issues, and staff estimates; for Honduras and Nicaragua, from IMF staff estimates; and for Tanzania, from the World Bank (1996f).

[1]Number of years between the preprogram year and the latest year for which data are available.

[2]Latest year is for the period 1993–95.

[3]For Bangladesh, Cambodia, and Nepal, data in column (2) are based on a two-year preprogram average instead of a three-year average.

[4]For Bolivia, data for the preprogram year are not available; instead, data from the first program year are presented in column (3).

[5]Due to data omissions, differences given in columns (5) and (6) for aggregated countries may not equal column differences.

Bibliography

Alderman, Harold, Jere R. Behrman, Shahrukh Khan, David R. Ross, and Richard Sabot, 1995, "Public Schooling Expenditures in Rural Pakistan: Efficiently Targeting Girls and a Lagging Region," in *Public Spending and the Poor: Theory and Evidence,* ed. by Dominique van de Walle and Kimberly Nead (Baltimore: Johns Hopkins University Press), pp. 187–222.

Amjadi, Azita, Ulrich Reincke, and Alexander J. Yeats, 1996, "Did External Barriers Cause the Marginalization of Sub-Saharan Africa in World Trade?" World Bank Policy Research Paper No. 1586 (Washington: World Bank).

Casanegra de Jantscher, Milka, and Richard M. Bird, 1992, "The Reform of Tax Administration," in *Improving Tax Administration in Developing Countries,* ed. by Richard M. Bird and Milka Casanegra de Jantscher (Washington: International Monetary Fund), pp. 1–18.

Castro-Leal, Dayton, and Lionel Demery, forthcoming, "Benefits Incidence of Social Spending: Inter-Country Comparison," World Bank Public Spending and Poverty Series (Washington: World Bank).

Cheasty, Adrienne, and Jeffrey M. Davis, 1996, "Fiscal Transition in Countries of the Former Soviet Union: An Interim Assessment," *MOCT-MOST,* Vol. 6 (No. 3), pp. 7–34.

Chu, Ke-young, and Sanjeev Gupta, 1996, "Social Protection in Transition Countries: Emerging Issues," IMF Paper on Policy Analysis and Assessment 96/5 (Washington: International Monetary Fund).

———, Benedict Clements, Daniel Hewitt, Sergio Lugaresi, Jerald Schiff, Ludger Schuknecht, and Gerd Schwartz, 1995, *Unproductive Public Expenditures: A Pragmatic Approach to Policy Analysis,* IMF Pamphlet Series, No. 48 (Washington: Fiscal Affairs Department, International Monetary Fund).

Clément, Jean A.P., Johannes Mueller, Stéphane Cossé, and Jean LeDem, 1996, *Aftermath of the CFA Franc Devaluation,* IMF Occasional Paper No. 138 (Washington: International Monetary Fund).

Cornély, Jean-Paul, 1995, "Conditions for the Success of a VAT in Africa," paper presented at Symposium Coopération Française–World Bank–IMF, Washington, May 2–4 (unpublished; Washington: International Monetary Fund).

Dean, Judith Myrle, Seema Desai, and James Riedel, 1994, *Trade Policy Reform in Developing Countries Since 1985: A Review of the Evidence* (Washington: World Bank).

Deininger, Klaus, and Lyn Squire, 1996, "A New Data Set Measuring Income Inequality," *World Bank Economic Review,* Vol. 10 (September), pp. 565–91.

Dia, Mamadou, 1993, "A Governance Approach to Civil Service Reform in Sub-Saharan Africa," World Bank Technical Paper No. 225, Africa Technical Department Series (Washington: World Bank).

Grosh, Margaret E., 1994, *Administering Targeted Social Programs in Latin America: From Platitudes to Practice* (Washington: World Bank).

Gupta, Sanjeev, Jerald Schiff, and Benedict Clements, 1996, "Worldwide Military Spending, 1990–95," IMF Working Paper 96/64 (Washington: International Monetary Fund).

International Monetary Fund, forthcoming, *The ESAF at Ten Years: Economic Adjustment and Reform in Low-Income Countries* (Washington: IMF).

Jayarajah, Carl A.B., William H. Branson, and Binayak Sen, 1996, *Social Dimensions of Adjustment: World Bank Experience, 1980–93* (Washington: World Bank).

Jorgensen, Steen, Margaret Grosh, and Mark Schacter, eds., 1992, *Bolivia's Answer to Poverty, Economic Crisis, and Adjustments: The Emergency Social Fund* (Washington: World Bank).

Kraay, Aart, and Caroline Van Rijckeghem, 1995, "Employment and Wages in the Public Sector—A Cross-Country Study," IMF Working Paper 95/70 (Washington: International Monetary Fund).

Mackenzie, G.A., David W.H. Orsmond, and Philip R. Gerson, 1997, *The Composition of Fiscal Adjustment and Growth: Lessons from Fiscal Reforms in Eight Economies,* IMF Occasional Paper No. 149 (Washington: International Monetary Fund).

Nashashibi, Karim, Sanjeev Gupta, Claire Liuksila, Henri Lorie, and Walter Mahler, 1992, *The Fiscal Dimensions of Adjustment in Low-Income Countries,* IMF Occasional Paper No. 95 (Washington: International Monetary Fund).

Ng, Francis, and Alexander Yeats, 1997, "Open Economies Work Better! Did Africa's Protectionist Policies Cause Its Marginalization in World Trade?" World Bank Policy Research Working Paper No. 1636 (Washington: World Bank).

Nunberg, Barbara, and John Nellis, 1995, "Civil Service Reform and the World Bank," World Bank Discussion Paper No. 161 (Washington: World Bank).

Petrei, A. Humberto, 1987, "El Gasto Público Social y sus Efectos Distribuidos: Un Examen Comparativo de Cinco Países de América Latina," ECIEL Document Series No. 7 (Río de Janeiro: Programa de Estudios Conjuntos sobre Integración Económica Latinoamericana).

———, 1996, "Distribución del Ingreso: El Papel del Gasto Público Social," Serie Política Fiscal No. 81 (Santiago: UN, CEPAL).

Schiavo-Campo, Salvatore, Giulio de Tommaso, and Amitabha Mukherjee, 1997a, "Government Employment and Pay: A Global and Regional Perspective," background paper for *World Development Report,* World Bank Policy Research Working Paper No. 1771 (Washington: World Bank).

———, 1997b, "An International Statistical Survey of Government Employment and Wages," background paper for *World Development Report,* World Bank Policy Research Working Paper No. 1806 (Washington: World Bank).

Schwartz, Gerd, and Teresa Ter-Minassian, 1995, "The Distributional Effects of Public Expenditure: Update and Overview," IMF Working Paper 95/84 (Washington: International Monetary Fund).

Shome, Parthasarathi, ed., 1995, *Tax Policy Handbook* (Washington: Tax Policy Division, Fiscal Affairs Department, International Monetary Fund).

Stotsky, Janet G., and Asegedech WoldeMariam, 1997, "Tax Effort in Sub-Saharan Africa," IMF Working Paper 97/107 (Washington: International Monetary Fund).

Tait, Alan A., Wilfrid L.M. Grätz, and Barry J. Eichengreen, 1979, "International Comparisons of Taxation for Selected Developing Countries, 1972–76," *Staff Papers,* International Monetary Fund, Vol. 26 (March), pp. 123–56.

Tanzi, Vito, 1987, "Quantitative Characteristics of the Tax Systems of Developing Countries," in *The Theory of Taxation for Developing Countries,* ed. by David M.G. Newbery and Nicholas Herbert Stern (New York: Oxford University Press for the World Bank), pp. 205–41.

———, 1992, "Structural Factors and Tax Revenue in Developing Countries: A Decade of Evidence," in *Open Economies: Structural Adjustment and Agriculture,* ed. by Ian Goldin and L. Alan Winters (Cambridge: Cambridge University Press), pp. 267–85.

———, and Anthony J. Pellechio, 1995, "The Reform of Tax Administration," IMF Working Paper 95/22 (Washington: International Monetary Fund).

Tanzi, Vito, and Ludger Schuknecht, 1995, "The Growth of Government and the Reform of the State in Industrial Countries," IMF Working Paper 95/130 (Washington: International Monetary Fund).

van de Walle, Dominique, 1995, "Incidence and Targeting: An Overview of Implications for Research and Policy," in *Public Spending and the Poor: Theory and Evidence,* ed. by Dominique van de Walle and Kimberly Nead (Baltimore: Johns Hopkins University Press), pp. 585–619.

World Bank, 1996a, *Bangladesh–Public Expenditure Review,* Report No. 15905 (Washington: World Bank).

———, 1996b, *Bolivia–Poverty, Equity, and Income: Selected Policies for Expanding Earning Opportunities for the Poor,* Report No. 15272-BO, Vols. 1–2 (Washington: World Bank).

———, 1996c, *Madagascar–Poverty Assessment,* Report No. 14044, Vols. 1–2 (Washington: World Bank).

———, 1996d, *Summary of Poverty Reduction and the World Bank: Progress and Challenges in the 1990s* (Washington: World Bank).

———, 1996e, *Tanzania–The Challenge of Reforms: Growth, Incomes, and Welfare,* Report No. 14982, Vols. 1–3 (Washington: World Bank).

———, 1996f, *Uganda: The Challenge of Growth and Poverty Reduction,* World Bank Country Study 0253-2123 (Washington: World Bank).

———, 1997, *Poverty in Côte d'Ivoire,* Sector Report No. 15640 (Washington: World Bank).

Recent Occasional Papers of the International Monetary Fund

160. Fiscal Reform in Low-Income Countries: Experience Under IMF-Supported Programs, by a Staff Team led by George T. Abed. 1998.

159. Hungary: Economic Policies for Sustainable Growth, Carlo Cottarelli, Thomas Krueger, Reza Moghadam, Perry Perone, Edgardo Ruggiero, and Rachel van Elkan. 1998

158. Transparency in Goverment Operations, by George Kopits and Jon Craig. 1998

157. Central Bank Reforms in the Baltics, Russia, and the Other Countries of the Former Soviet Union, by a Staff Team led by Malcolm Knight and comprising Susana Almuiña, John Dalton, Inci Otker, Ceyla Pazarbaşıoğlu, Arne B. Petersen, Peter Quirk, Nicholas M. Roberts, Gabriel Sensenbrenner, and Jan Willem van der Vossen. 1997.

156. The ESAF at Ten Years: Economic Adjustment and Reform in Low-Income Countries, by the Staff of the International Monetary Fund. 1997.

155. Fiscal Policy Issues During the Transition in Russia, by Augusto Lopez-Claros and Sergei Alexashenko. 1998.

154. Credibility Without Rules? Monetary Frameworks in the Post–Bretton Woods Era, by Carlo Cottarelli and Curzio Giannini. 1997.

153. Pension Regimes and Saving, by G.A. Mackenzie, Philip Gerson, and Alfredo Cuevas. 1997.

152. Hong Kong, China: Growth, Structural Change, and Economic Stability During the Transition, by John Dodsworth and Dubravko Mihaljek. 1997.

151. Currency Board Arrangements: Issues and Experiences, by a staff team led by Tomás J.T. Baliño and Charles Enoch. 1997.

150. Kuwait: From Reconstruction to Accumulation for Future Generations, by Nigel Andrew Chalk, Mohamed A. El-Erian, Susan J. Fennell, Alexei P. Kireyev, and John F. Wison. 1997.

149. The Composition of Fiscal Adjustment and Growth: Lessons from Fiscal Reforms in Eight Economies, by G.A. Mackenzie, David W.H. Orsmond, and Philip R. Gerson. 1997.

148. Nigeria: Experience with Structural Adjustment, by Gary Moser, Scott Rogers, and Reinold van Til, with Robin Kibuka and Inutu Lukonga. 1997.

147. Aging Populations and Public Pension Schemes, by Sheetal K. Chand and Albert Jaeger. 1996.

146. Thailand: The Road to Sustained Growth, by Kalpana Kochhar, Louis Dicks-Mireaux, Balazs Horvath, Mauro Mecagni, Erik Offerdal, and Jianping Zhou. 1996.

145. Exchange Rate Movements and Their Impact on Trade and Investment in the APEC Region, by Takatoshi Ito, Peter Isard, Steven Symansky, and Tamim Bayoumi. 1996.

144. National Bank of Poland: The Road to Indirect Instruments, by Piero Ugolini. 1996.

143. Adjustment for Growth: The African Experience, by Michael T. Hadjimichael, Michael Nowak, Robert Sharer, and Amor Tahari. 1996.

142. Quasi-Fiscal Operations of Public Financial Institutions, by G.A. Mackenzie and Peter Stella. 1996.

141. Monetary and Exchange System Reforms in China: An Experiment in Gradualism, by Hassanali Mehran, Marc Quintyn, Tom Nordman, and Bernard Laurens. 1996.

140. Government Reform in New Zealand, by Graham C. Scott. 1996.

139. Reinvigorating Growth in Developing Countries: Lessons from Adjustment Policies in Eight Economies, by David Goldsbrough, Sharmini Coorey, Louis Dicks-Mireaux, Balazs Horvath, Kalpana Kochhar, Mauro Mecagni, Erik Offerdal, and Jianping Zhou. 1996.

138. Aftermath of the CFA Franc Devaluation, by Jean A.P. Clément, with Johannes Mueller, Stéphane Cossé, and Jean Le Dem. 1996.

137. The Lao People's Democratic Republic: Systemic Transformation and Adjustment, edited by Ichiro Otani and Chi Do Pham. 1996.

136. Jordan: Strategy for Adjustment and Growth, edited by Edouard Maciejewski and Ahsan Mansur. 1996.

135. Vietnam: Transition to a Market Economy, by John R. Dodsworth, Erich Spitäller, Michael Braulke, Keon Hyok Lee, Kenneth Miranda, Christian Mulder, Hisanobu Shishido, and Krishna Srinivasan. 1996.

134. India: Economic Reform and Growth, by Ajai Chopra, Charles Collyns, Richard Hemming, and Karen Parker with Woosik Chu and Oliver Fratzscher. 1995.

133. Policy Experiences and Issues in the Baltics, Russia, and Other Countries of the Former Soviet Union, edited by Daniel A. Citrin and Ashok K. Lahiri. 1995.

132. Financial Fragilities in Latin America: The 1980s and 1990s, by Liliana Rojas-Suárez and Steven R. Weisbrod. 1995.

131. Capital Account Convertibility: Review of Experience and Implications for IMF Policies, by staff teams headed by Peter J. Quirk and Owen Evans. 1995.

130. Challenges to the Swedish Welfare State, by Desmond Lachman, Adam Bennett, John H. Green, Robert Hagemann, and Ramana Ramaswamy. 1995.

129. IMF Conditionality: Experience Under Stand-By and Extended Arrangements. Part II: Background Papers. Susan Schadler, Editor, with Adam Bennett, Maria Carkovic, Louis Dicks-Mireaux, Mauro Mecagni, James H.J. Morsink, and Miguel A. Savastano. 1995.

128. IMF Conditionality: Experience Under Stand-By and Extended Arrangements. Part I: Key Issues and Findings, by Susan Schadler, Adam Bennett, Maria Carkovic, Louis Dicks-Mireaux, Mauro Mecagni, James H.J. Morsink, and Miguel A. Savastano. 1995.

127. Road Maps of the Transition: The Baltics, the Czech Republic, Hungary, and Russia, by Biswajit Banerjee, Vincent Koen, Thomas Krueger, Mark S. Lutz, Michael Marrese, and Tapio O. Saavalainen. 1995.

126. The Adoption of Indirect Instruments of Monetary Policy, by a staff team headed by William E. Alexander, Tomás J.T. Baliño, and Charles Enoch. 1995.

125. United Germany: The First Five Years—Performance and Policy Issues, by Robert Corker, Robert A. Feldman, Karl Habermeier, Hari Vittas, and Tessa van der Willigen. 1995.

124. Saving Behavior and the Asset Price "Bubble" in Japan: Analytical Studies, edited by Ulrich Baumgartner and Guy Meredith. 1995.

123. Comprehensive Tax Reform: The Colombian Experience, edited by Parthasarathi Shome. 1995.

122. Capital Flows in the APEC Region, edited by Mohsin S. Khan and Carmen M. Reinhart. 1995.

121. Uganda: Adjustment with Growth, 1987–94, by Robert L. Sharer, Hema R. De Zoysa, and Calvin A. McDonald. 1995.

120. Economic Dislocation and Recovery in Lebanon, by Sena Eken, Paul Cashin, S. Nuri Erbas, Jose Martelino, and Adnan Mazarei. 1995.

119. Singapore: A Case Study in Rapid Development, edited by Kenneth Bercuson with a staff team comprising Robert G. Carling, Aasim M. Husain, Thomas Rumbaugh, and Rachel van Elkan. 1995.

118. Sub-Saharan Africa: Growth, Savings, and Investment, by Michael T. Hadjimichael, Dhaneshwar Ghura, Martin Mühleisen, Roger Nord, and E. Murat Uçer. 1995.

117. Resilience and Growth Through Sustained Adjustment: The Moroccan Experience, by Saleh M. Nsouli, Sena Eken, Klaus Enders, Van-Can Thai, Jörg Decressin, and Filippo Cartiglia, with Janet Bungay. 1995.

116. Improving the International Monetary System: Constraints and Possibilities, by Michael Mussa, Morris Goldstein, Peter B. Clark, Donald J. Mathieson, and Tamim Bayoumi. 1994.

115. Exchange Rates and Economic Fundamentals: A Framework for Analysis, by Peter B. Clark, Leonardo Bartolini, Tamim Bayoumi, and Steven Symansky. 1994.

114. Economic Reform in China: A New Phase, by Wanda Tseng, Hoe Ee Khor, Kalpana Kochhar, Dubravko Mihaljek, and David Burton. 1994.

Note: For information on the title and availability of Occasional Papers not listed, please consult the IMF Publications Catalog or contact IMF Publication Services.